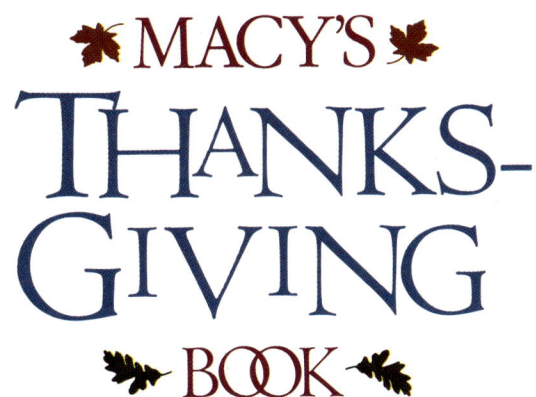

MACY'S THANKS-GIVING BOOK

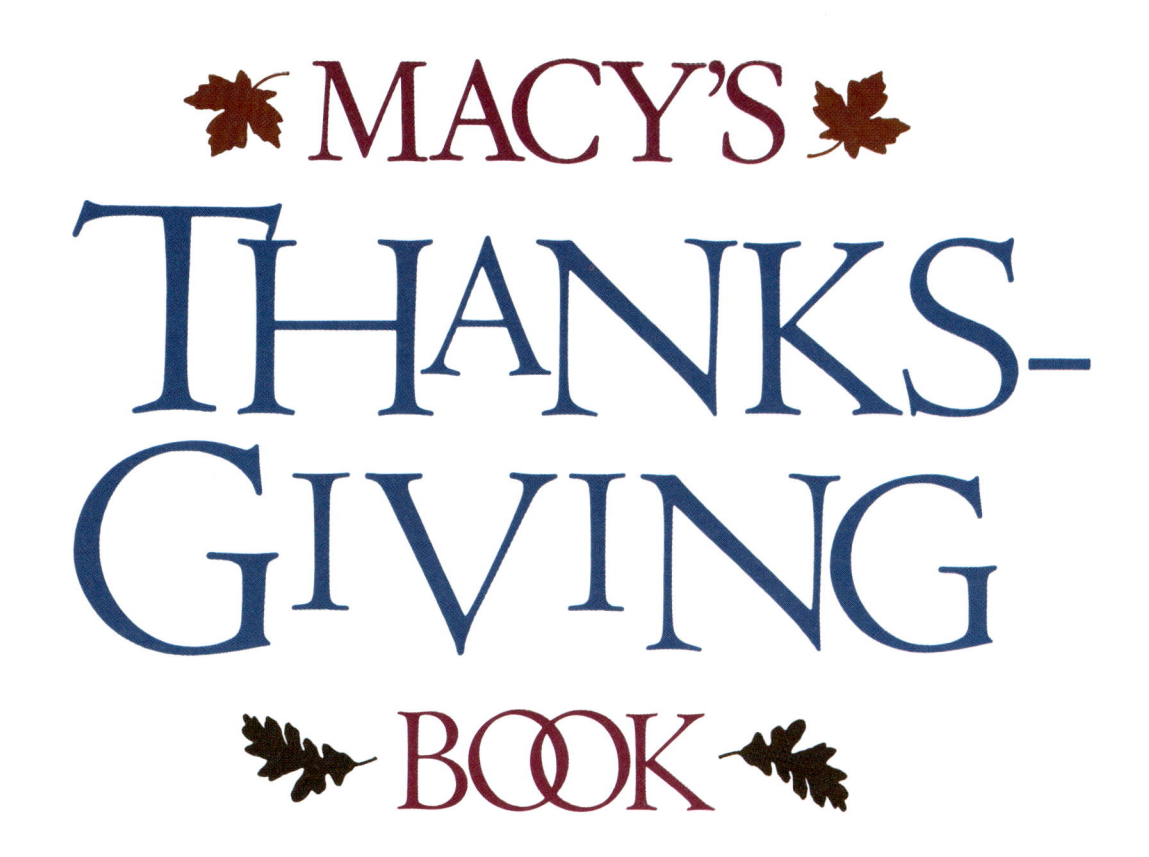

Consulting Editor Naomi Black

The Tradition and *Macy's Parade* by Meg Crager
Fun-Filled Activities and Traditions to Establish by Margaret Grace
The Celebration by Jamie Harrison
Festive Crafts by Andrea Soorikian
Song Adaptations by Elizabeth Grossman

A QUARTO BOOK
RUNNING PRESS
BOOK PUBLISHERS
PHILADELPHIA, PENNSYLVANIA

A QUARTO BOOK

Copyright© 1986 by Quarto Marketing Ltd.

All rights reserved. No part of this publication
may be reproduced, stored in a retrieval system,
or transmitted, in any form or by any means,
electronic, mechanical, photocopying, recording,
or otherwise, without the prior written permission
of the copyright owner.

9 8 7 6 5 4 3 2 1

Digit on the right indicates the number of this printing.

Library of Congress Cataloging in Publication Number
GT4975.M32 1986   394.2'683   86-10072

ISBN 0-89471-467-8

MACY'S THANKSGIVING BOOK
was prepared and produced by
Quarto Marketing Ltd.
15 West 26th Street
New York, N.Y. 10010

Macy's is a federally registered trademark of R. H. Macy and Co., Inc.

Designer: Robert Kosturko
Photo Researcher: Susan M. Duane
Production Manager: Karen L. Greenberg

Typeset by I, CLAVDIA Phototypesetting & Graphic Design Inc.
Color separations by South Seas Graphic Art Company
Printed and bound in Hong Kong by Leefung-Asco Printers Ltd.
Cover photograph by Matthew Klein
Styling by Linda Cheverton and Andrea Swenson
Photo Production: Susan M. Duane

This book may be ordered from the publisher
Please include $1.00 postage
But try your bookstore first.

Running Press Book Publishers
125 South 22nd Street
Philadelphia, Pennsylvania 19103

ACKNOWLEDGMENTS

The editor gratefully acknowledges the following people for granting permission to print their recipes:

Andreé Abramoff, owner and chef of Andreé's Mediterranean Cuisine restaurant of New York City.

The estate of James Beard.

Bert Greene, author of *Greene on Greens* (Workman), *Bert Greene's Kitchen Bouquets* (Contemporary Books), and *Honest American Fare* (Contemporary Books), among others.

Jamie Harrison, food writer and freelance caterer with Harrison-West.

Abe de la Houssaye, chef and owner of Texarkana and La Louisiana restaurants of New York City.

Richard Lavin, chef and owner of Lavin's restaurant of New York City.

Lydie Marshall, director of A La Bonne Cocotte cooking school in New York City.

Perla Meyers, author of *The Seasonal Kitchen* (Vintage Books), *The Peasant Kitchen* (Vintage Books), and *From Market to Kitchen* (Harper & Row).

Jean-Louis Palladin, chef of Jean-Louis restaurant in the Watergate Hotel of Washington, DC.

Alain Sailhac, chef de cuisine of Le Cirque restaurant of New York City.

Dieter Schorner, executive pastry chef of Tavern on the Green restaurant of New York City.

Thanks are also due to:

Chamber of Commerce of Plymouth, MA

Arlene Feltman of De Gustibus cooking school

Martha Friemond of Pilgrim Place

Linda Harrison

Kristi Kienholz of Old Sturbridge Village

The New York Botanical Garden Library

The New York City Convention and Visitors Bureau

The New-York Historical Society

Karla Olson

Kyle Roderick

Matthew Klein

and
Special thanks to
Our friends at Macy's

CONTENTS

Introduction
PAGE 8

The Tradition
PAGE 10

Thanksgiving through the Years
PAGE 12

The Story of the First Thanksgiving
PAGE 20

Gourds, Sheaves, and Corn
PAGE 26

*Fun-Filled Activities and
Traditions to Establish*
PAGE 30

Macy's Parade
PAGE 34

A Tradition Is Born
PAGE 36

Balloons
PAGE 46

Floats, Celebrities, and Bands
PAGE 56

The Celebration
PAGE 64

A Traditional Thanksgiving Meal
PAGE 66

CONTENTS

Dishes from Eras Past
PAGE 72

A Holiday Buffet
PAGE 76

Regional Specialties
PAGE 80

The Children's Corner
PAGE 84

Luscious Leftovers
PAGE 88

Gifts to Bring
PAGE 91

De Gustibus – Macy's Cooking School
PAGE 94

Festive Crafts
PAGE 98

A Thanksgiving Anthology
PAGE 110

Bibliography
PAGE 154

Food Sources
PAGE 155

Index
PAGE 157

Introduction

The Macy's Thanksgiving Book is designed to help you and your family experience the holiday at its best. We have included a fun-filled parade "guidebook," stories and poems to be read aloud to young children, songs for the whole family to sing, crafts to decorate the house for the season, and recipes to make your Thanksgiving guests return year after year. *The Macy's Thanksgiving Book* contains a wealth of ideas, brimming with originality and tradition—all gathered together under one cover for making the holiday a spirited time of warmth and happiness.

THE TRADITION was put together with the young reader in mind. From The Story of the First Thanksgiving to Gourds, Sheaves, and Corn, this collection goes behind the traditions and offers tales that explain them. You'll learn how to set up a harvest table, what Indian corn meant to the first settlers, and why sheaves of wheat have become a traditional symbol of the autumn.

MACY'S PARADE celebrates the big event of the holiday. Whether you watch it on television or from the sidewalks of New York City, you'll feel as if you're a part of the parade itself after having read these pages. You'll find out which hotels offer the best views of the procession, how the parade is planned, what the balloons are made of and how they're inflated. The pictures alone will keep children captivated and remembering the happy day long after it has passed.

THE CELEBRATION tantalizes its readers with pages of mouthwatering recipes: currant stuffing, wild rice with chanterelles and fresh chives, pear-and-cranberry compote, bread pudding with bourbon sauce, and more. If you want to leave the tried-and-true turkey behind, you can try the duck breasts with apples cooked in applejack, the roast goose, or roast capon recipes. And the children will be delighted with their own glazed ham, twice-baked potatoes, applesauce, and gingerbread. Take your choice, there are menus here for a number of meals: traditional, historical, regional, and buffet. Of course, you'll want to look into the leftovers and gifts sections too.

To round out THE CELEBRATION, Macy's and its famous De Gustibus Cooking School provide a sampling of extra-special recipes from some of the most renowned chefs in the United States.

FESTIVE CRAFTS complements the good helpings of Thanksgiving food; these pages open up to reveal delicate centerpieces and side-table arrangements, a bright parade table setting for the kids, and activities for the whole family. Fresh and simple, the ideas are designed for people who want beautiful results in no time at all.

Once you've decorated the house and have the food preparation underway, take time out to have a singalong or story hour. Steeped in oral and written traditions, Thanksgiving is a day of song and merriment as well as a time for reflection and giving thanks for all that's good in the world. A THANKSGIVING ANTHOLOGY read out loud will help to bring adults and children—the whole gathering—together. After all, isn't that what Thanksgiving is all about?

Thanksgiving, like most other holidays, offers quite a treasure trove of ideas for decorating the home, using turkey and harvest motifs, pilgrims, and the grand Macy's parade as inspiration. The projects included here require only basic skills: machine sewing, simple embroidery, and basic construction techniques. These ideas can bring out the artist in everyone—from the child putting together his or her first pomander ball to the father who while making the parade centerpiece decides to adapt it a little to match a favorite float from years before. When finished, these crafts will come to life and add joy to your holiday home.

The Tradition

Thanksgiving through the Years

Throughout history, people have celebrated and given thanks at harvest time. A good harvest meant plentiful food, and plentiful food ensured the continuity of life.

The ancient Greeks had a special festival for Demeter, their goddess of the harvest. The Romans celebrated Cerelia in honor of Ceres, their goddess of corn. The Anglo-Saxon Harvest Home was a day of great celebration; after the last cartload of grain was brought in, the landowners served a feast to all their farm workers. Sukkoth, a Jewish holiday is a similar celebration, a time of thanks for the harvest.

The Feast of St. Martin of Tours was celebrated in Europe in the Middle Ages. This festival was held in honor of filled barns and stocked larders. On the morning of Martinmas, everyone attended mass to give thanks for the harvest. In the afternoon, villagers enjoyed a great feast that featured a roast goose.

The first American harvest festival was celebrated in 1621 by the Pilgrims in Plymouth, Massachusetts. This

The first American harvest festival was celebrated by the Pilgrims of Plymouth, Massachusetts in 1621.

celebration has come to be known as the first Thanksgiving. However, while such a harvest feast did actually take place in Plymouth, it was only a feast, not a time of thanksgiving for the Pilgrims. Among the Pilgrims were Puritans, highly religious men and women who believed that festivities and games were delightful pastimes but should be kept separate from prayer. Thus, they had other religious days of thanksgiving, when they gave thanks to God and ate a simple meal. For example, when a drought destroyed their crops in the spring of 1623, they held a full day of fasting and prayer for rain. When the rain came, they had a thanksgiving day, which was a day of grateful prayer and religious rejoicing.

A pattern of religious fasting and feasting became part of the New England way of life for over a hundred years. Whenever they were faced with severe difficulties or dangers, the religious New Englanders set aside a special day for prayer and fasting. When their prayers were answered, they held a day of thanksgiving. Such events as success in battle and deliverance from drought, flood, hurricane, and illness were cause for thanksgiving days.

The New Amsterdam Dutch had similar days of prayer, called Fasting Prayer and Thanksgiving Days, or simply Thank Days. Unlike the Puritan New Englanders, however, the Dutch didn't feel it was wrong to mix prayer and secular celebration. Thank Days began with several hours of prayer and fasting and ended with celebrations and feasting. Celebrations were noisy, joyous affairs with military displays, games, and the firing of cannons.

Until 1789 each state fixed the date of its annual thanksgiving days. In New England, a pattern of fast and thanksgiving days developed: Fast days were held in the spring, and thanksgiving days were held in the fall.

During the American Revolution, the Continental Congress called for several national thanksgiving days for victories over the British. In 1778 George Washington proclaimed a day of thanks for the treaties made with France. In 1789 he issued a proclamation for a national thanksgiving on November 26. The next national thanksgiving was called for by President Madison to celebrate an era of peace after the War of 1812. These thanksgiving days were singular events; the idea of an annual national holiday had not yet caught on.

New Englanders, however, celebrated the harvest each year. They lost some of their religious intensity and were willing

Macy's Thanksgiving Book

to combine religious thanksgiving with an autumn harvest feast. By the early nineteenth century, they were celebrating Thanksgiving as we now know it. Here's a description of a typical nineteenth-century New England farm celebration.

On a cool day in late November—the day before the Thanksgiving feast—relatives from out of town began to arrive in their buggies at the big white farmhouse on top of the hill. The host and hostess welcomed them at the door. The largest turkey had been fattened and the pumpkins had ripened in the sun. The best garden vegetables, apples, pears, and cranberries had been set aside specifically for the Thanksgiving dinner. In the afternoon, the children played games and made popcorn while their mothers tended the turkey in the oven and the contents of bubbling pots on the stove. In the evening the whole family gathered for supper. Afterward everyone sat around the fireplace to listen to the older generation tell stories of the past.

On Thanksgiving morning, everyone attended church services. The minister gave a special Thanksgiving sermon, speaking of the many things his parishioners had to be thankful for. On their way home, the family often encountered groups of poor children dressed in costumes, begging for food and money for their families. The father of the family would give the poor children some money, as charity was part of the New England Thanksgiving tradition. Before dinner, the men went out to the woods for a turkey-shooting match. Finally it was time to enjoy the Thanksgiving feast.

This celebration of Thanksgiving began in New England. But as New Englanders moved west to the frontier states, they brought their customs with them. For example, in Iowa in the 1840s, farms were producing bumper crops, and the settlers were delighted to adopt the Thanksgiving custom. In 1844 Governor John Chambers drafted a Thanksgiving manifesto calling for the first official Iowa Thanksgiving. As a result of its popularity, the custom spread west. San Francisco had its first Thanksgiving in 1847, and in 1875, Los Angeles held its first official Thanksgiving.

A woman named Sarah Josepha Hale was greatly responsible for the advent of a national Thanksgiving. She was the editor of *Godey's Lady's Book,* the most widely read American periodical of the era. She believed that Thanksgiving was a time for family reunions and an opportunity to strengthen and renew American patriotism. She embarked on an almost thirty-year campaign to make it a national holiday. Over the years she sent letters to all the governors of the states and territories and to each president. As a result, many governors issued Thanksgiving proclamations.

In 1863 President Abraham Lincoln issued the first national Thanksgiving Day proclamation. He called for a nationwide celebration on the last Thursday in November. The Civil War had split the country—it was just after the northern victory at Gettysburg, Pennsylvania—and Lincoln's proclamation asked that all Americans pray for "those who have become widows, orphans, or mourners, or sufferers in the lamentable civil strife in which we are unavoidably engaged." He also asked all Americans to pray to God to heal the wounds of the nation.

It has seemed to me fit and proper that they should be solemnly, reverently and gratefully acknowledged as with one heart and one voice by the whole American people. I do, therefor, invite my fellow citizens in every part of the United States, and also those who are at sea and those who are sojourning in foreign lands, to set apart and observe the last Thursday of November next as a day of thanksgiving and praise to our beneficent Father who dwelleth in the heavens.

—ABRAHAM LINCOLN
OCTOBER 3, 1863

A turkey-shooting match was one of the traditional events of Thanksgiving in eighteenth-century New England.

historic homes. Each Thanksgiving the villagers of Plimouth Plantation stage a play and attend church services. Following these events is a public Thanksgiving Day dinner. (For more information contact the Plymouth Area Chamber of Commerce at 617–746–3377.)

At Old Sturbridge Village, a living history museum that recreates an 1830s New England town, in Sturbridge, Massachusetts, costumed interpreters recreate an early nineteenth-century New England Thanksgiving. Cooking preparations go on throughout the week just as they did in the 1830s: pie baking, turkey trussing and roasting, and preparing vegetables that were harvested there at the village. Breads, mince pies, cranberry sauce, and Marlborough pudding await the table. Costumed interpreters talk with visitors about early nineteenth-century recipes and holiday customs.

As Thanksgiving Day approaches, the variety of activities increases. On the Saturday before Thanksgiving, Old Sturbridge Village holds a competitive turkey shoot. Historically dressed villagers demonstrate their skill by aiming at paper targets, which in the past were sometimes used instead of live birds. On Thanksgiving Day, the foods are displayed in the village houses. Visitors may attend meetinghouse services, and in the late afternoon, elegantly dressed interpreters demonstrate early nineteenth-century dances.

On the three-day weekend after Thanksgiving, special hands-on activities are offered, which provide visitors with the opportunity to do some of the tasks and use implements of the 1830s. (For more information contact Old Sturbridge Village at 617–347–3362.)

Another Thanksgiving attraction is Pilgrim Place in Claremont, California, a community of retired missionaries and other Christian workers. Each November the residents hold a special Pilgrim Festival that includes a historical pageant about the Pilgrims and the first settlement at Plymouth, a crafts fair, and a turkey luncheon. (For more information contact Pilgrim Place at 714–621–9581.)

Reservations for Thanksgiving at these and other historic communities should be made several months in advance.

At Old Sturbridge Village in Sturbridge, Massachusetts, costumed interpreters recreate an early nineteenth-century New England Thanksgiving. Activities include a turkey shoot, meetinghouse services, and music and dancing of the era.

Many historic homes and villages around the country reenact old-fashioned Thanksgivings.

Commonwealth of  Massachusetts.

BY HIS EXCELLENCY
JOHN A. ANDREW,
GOVERNOR:
A PROCLAMATION.

WHEREAS, The President of the United States of America did by his Proclamation, Dated at Washington, on the fifteenth day of July current, "set apart THURSDAY, the sixth day of August next to be observed as a day for National Thanksgiving, Praise and Prayer," in recognition of the wonderful things done by the Divine Majesty in behalf of this Nation:

I do therefore direct and request that the aforesaid Proclamation of the Chief Executive Magistrate of the United States be published and promulgated to the people of Massachusetts in the same manner in which the Proclamation of the Governor of Massachusetts is accustomed to be promulgated, ordaining the Annual Thanksgiving observed in this Commonwealth.

I earnestly trust not only that in all our Churches and Congregations of religious worship the day may be observed by becoming acts of public thanksgiving, but that every heart may find an altar on which to lay its offering of humble and grateful praise.

Given at the Council Chamber, in Boston, this twenty-seventh day of July, in the year one thousand eight hundred and sixty-three, and the eighty-eighth of the Independence of the United States.

JOHN A. ANDREW.

BY HIS EXCELLENCY THE GOVERNOR:
OLIVER WARNER, *Secretary.*

God Save the Commonwealth of Massachusetts.

BY HIS EXCELLENCY
ABRAHAM LINCOLN,
PRESIDENT OF THE UNITED STATES OF AMERICA:
A PROCLAMATION
For a Day of Thanksgiving, Praise, and Prayer.

It has pleased Almighty God to hearken to supplications and prayers of an afflicted people, and to vouchsafe to the Army and Navy of the United States on the land and on the sea, victories so signal and so effective as to furnish reasonable grounds for augmented confidence, that the Union of these States will be maintained, their constitution preserved, and peace and prosperity permanently established; but these victories have been accorded not without sacrifice of life, limb, health, and liberty, incurred by brave, patriotic and loyal citizens. Domestic affliction in every part of the country follows in the train of these fearful bereavements.

It is meet and right to recognize and confess the presence of the Almighty Father and the power of His hand equally in these triumphs and these sorrows.

Now, therefore, be it known, that I do set apart, THURSDAY, THE SIXTH DAY OF AUGUST NEXT, to be observed as a day for National Thanksgiving, Praise and Prayer; and I invite the people of the United States to assemble on that occasion in their customary places of worship, and in the forms approved by their own conscience, render the homage due to the Divine Majesty for the wonderful things he has done in the Nation's behalf, and invoke the influence of His holy spirit to subdue the anger, which has produced and so long sustained a needless rebellion; to change the hearts of the insurgents, to guide the counsels of the government with wisdom adequate to so great a national emergency, and to visit with tender care and consolation throughout the length and breadth of our land all those who through the vicissitudes of marches, voyages, battles, and sieges have been brought to suffer in mind, body, or estate; and finally, to lead the whole Nation, through paths of repentance and submission to the Divine will, back to the perfect enjoyment of Union and fraternal peace.

In witness whereof I have hereunto set my hand and caused the seal of the United States to be affixed. Done at the City of Washington this fifteenth day of July, one thousand eight hundred and sixty-three, and of the Independence of the United States of America, the eighty-eighth.

ABRAHAM LINCOLN.

BY THE PRESIDENT:
WILLIAM H. SEWARD, *Secretary of State.*

Sarah Josepha Hale, editor of Godey's Lady's Book, *campaigned for a national Thanksgiving celebration for three decades. She wrote letters to the governors of all the states and territories, urging them to celebrate the special day.*

Since the historic proclamation of 1863 Thanksgiving has been observed around the country on the last Thursday in November. Lincoln, however, was not the last president to issue Thanksgiving addresses. In 1938 Franklin Delano Roosevelt gave a Thanksgiving message to the nation. Presidents Truman and Eisenhower also made Thanksgiving speeches.

By the mid-twentieth century, Thanksgiving had become so much a part of the American way of life that in 1942 American soldiers fighting in World War II celebrated Thanksgiving at London's Westminster Abbey. Special services were conducted by American army chaplains, and soldiers from all different branches of the armed forces, nurses, and Red Cross workers attended the service.

Thanksgiving is a day for family reunions and joyous celebrations all over the country; some customs are observed nationally, others regionally. The nationally televised Macy's Thanksgiving Day Parade is the morning's highlight for many families, especially those with young children. Many towns have special Thanksgiving footraces, known in some places as Turkey Trots. Even the Thanksgiving dinner varies from region to region. For example, a southwestern Thanksgiving might incorporate locally grown artichokes or avocados in the menu, or papaya in the fruit salad; the cranberry sauce served up North might be replaced by a pomegranate relish. Wherever it is served, Thanksgiving dinner is sure to be a feast.

Many historic homes and villages across the country hold special events for Thanksgiving. In Plymouth, Massachusetts, the Plimouth Plantation recreates the original Pilgrim village and its neighboring Wampanoag Indian camp. There, men and women demonstrate how the Pilgrims and the Indians lived and worked. Among the attractions are a full-scale replica of the *Mayflower* and reconstructions of the community's many

In 1863, during the Civil War, President Lincoln issued a proclamation calling for a national day of Thanksgiving. It has been a national holiday ever since.

Thanksgiving through the Years

The Story of the First Thanksgiving

The first American Thanksgiving was celebrated by the Pilgrims at Plymouth, Massachusetts, in 1621. The Pilgrims suffered many hardships on their way to the New World, and their first winter in America was very difficult. By the fall of 1621, however, they had good cause for celebration. In just one year, they had built a town in the wilderness; had learned to farm, fish, and hunt in the new land; had gathered a successful harvest; and were living in peace with the Indians.

The Puritans were a group of English religious dissidents who believed that religion should be based more on personal inspiration from God than on the teachings of a distant, hierarchical church. Because they publicized their beliefs, which called into question the whole political structure of England at the time, they were persecuted.

To avoid further persecution, they decided to move to Holland, where they could enjoy greater religious freedom. So they sold their farms, packed up their belongings, and traveled to Holland by boat. They soon settled

To escape persecution for their religious beliefs, the Puritans left England and settled in the Dutch city of Leyden. Before long, however, they decided to start their own new community in the New World.

Macy's Thanksgiving Book

The Mayflower carried 102 courageous men, women, and children across the ocean to the New World. The journey took sixty-six days.

The Pilgrims survived a difficult winter. In the spring, they were befriended by Squanto, a native who spoke English. He taught them the skills they needed to survive in the wilderness. By the fall, the Pilgrims had stored away enough food for the next winter, and could at last take time to enjoy the natural beauty of their new home.

in the picturesque Dutch city of Leiden. Before long, they found themselves the subjects of persecution once again.

A group of forty-one Puritans wanted to set out for the New World. There, they felt, they would truly be able to practice their religion in peace. At that time, the American continent was a vast wilderness that most Europeans knew very little about. There was a small English colony in Virginia, but only a few ships had explored the area that is now called New England. Imagine the courage of these men and women to set out across the ocean for the unknown!

The *Mayflower* carried a total of 102 passengers: 17 men and 10 women Puritans, 14 children, and 18 servants. The rest of the passengers were English people who were eager for adventure and a new life. The trip across the ocean took sixty-six days. The *Mayflower* landed at what is now known as Plymouth, Massachusetts, on November 11, 1620.

When they set foot on the new continent, the Pilgrims immediately said a prayer of thanksgiving to God for granting them a safe voyage. Then it was time to take care of practical matters. The men set out to gather wood, and the women washed the clothes and bedding and organized their belongings.

The captain, Miles Standish, led a group of men on an expedition to explore the new land. They walked several miles through the dense forest and although they found no houses, they discovered several caches of wheat, corn, and beans. They saw no one around, so they helped themselves to these much-needed supplies, which actually belonged to local Indians.

It was already wintertime in Plymouth, and very cold; everyone pitched in to build several rough wooden houses. The first building they put up served as a storehouse and meeting place. Then they built nineteen more shelters, enough to house all the *Mayflower*'s passengers. But the winter was crueler and colder than the Pilgrims were prepared for. They had barely enough to eat and lacked adequate supplies of such things as blankets and coats. Forty-seven of the *Mayflower*'s original 102 passengers died that winter from illness and starvation. But somehow, the Pilgrims managed to keep their hope. The six or seven people who stayed healthy tended the sick: They fetched wood, made fires, cooked food, made beds, and washed clothes. Most important of all, they spread cheerfulness to those who were suffering.

That spring brought warm weather and the Pilgrims' first friendly encounter with an Indian. One day, a man named Samo-

The Story of the First Thanksgiving

Preparations begin for a harvest celebration.

set walked into the settlement and greeted the Pilgrims in English. The settlers invited him to join them in their midday meal, and Samoset told them about himself in a combination of English and sign language. He lived nearby and, over the years, had met several English ship captains who had taught him a few words of the language. He told the Pilgrims about Squanto, another Indian who spoke much better English than he did. A few days later, Samoset returned with five of his tribesmen, who brought cornmeal and tobacco to the settlers.

On April 2, 1621, Samoset returned to Plymouth with Squanto, who spoke excellent English. He had lived for several years in England and was eager to help the settlers to survive in their new environment. He spent a great deal of time with them through the spring and summer, teaching them how to plant and fertilize corn, where to fish and hunt, and what kinds of wild fruits and vegetables to gather. They planted twenty acres of Indian corn and several more acres of English wheat and peas. The corn grew well, but the English seeds never sprouted, either because the seeds were not fertile or they were planted too late. The Pilgrims were grateful for Squanto's help because they had no previous experience in the wilderness.

Squanto also served as an interpreter and diplomat between the Pilgrims and the local Indians. On one occasion, he took a group that included William Bradford, governor of the colony, and some of the men of Plymouth to meet Massasoit, chief of the Wampanoag Indians. With Squanto's help the Indians and the Englishmen drew up a treaty, which established a fair and pragmatic agreement between them.

The settlers had a busy summer. Their main concern was to set aside more food and improve their shelter for the next winter. They spent their time tending the crops, and gathering and drying fish, fruit, and vegetables for the winter. They insulated the walls of their houses to keep out the cold and traded with the Indians for warm furs.

That fall, when the harvest had been gathered and stored away, the settlers planned a great celebration for themselves and their neighbors, the Wampanoag Indians.

Four men went out hunting while others gathered shellfish, fruits, and vegetables. All the settlers helped prepare for the celebration. They had been living on small amounts of rationed food since they left Europe, so they were very excited at the prospect of a feast. The women assembled days in advance to decide who

Squanto, Samoset, and Chief Massasoit and ninety of his men came to celebrate the harvest with the Pilgrims. The feast lasted three days. There was a great deal of eating and drinking, and contests of skill and marksmanship.

The Pilgrim women spent several days planning and preparing the great feast. They roasted wild turkey, venison, partridge, duck, and goose over an open flame.

The Story of the First Thanksgiving

would roast the game, prepare the fish, make the breads, and cook the vegetables. Even the youngest girls and boys were enlisted to help prepare the meal.

Huge wooden tables were set up in front of the houses. In attendance were fifty-five settlers and their guests, the Indians. Chief Massasoit came with ninety of his men and Squanto and Samoset were honored guests. The Indians did not come empty handed. They contributed five large deer, which they roasted on spits over a roaring fire. Everything was cooked in skillets, kettles, or over a hot and sizzling open flame.

Then it was time for the first Thanksgiving to begin. The children brought out pewter plates and knives. The women served huge steaming platters of mouth-watering food: hot fresh barley loaf, corn cakes, wild turkey, venison, partridge, duck, and roast goose. From the sea came clams, lobsters, cod, and bass. The garden fare included relishes and colorful cooked vegetables, fruit, and salad. Everything was washed down with wine made from wild grapes.

The food was delicious and plentiful, and the feast continued for three days. Other activities added to the festiveness. The Indians displayed their skills with the bow and arrow, and in turn, Captain Miles Standish and his militia gave a show of their marksmanship. There were footraces and relay races, jumping contests and shooting contests, and all around a feeling of great good will. After everyone had eaten, played, and enjoyed the festivities as much as was possible, the first Thanksgiving was over. Everyone agreed that the tradition of a wonderful celebration was established.

Gourds, Sheaves, and Corn

O rnamental gourds are one of the traditional symbols of the American Thanksgiving. A basketful of colorful gourds will bring a touch of harvesttime to the home. If you have a garden, you'll find that they're easy to grow. If you don't have a garden, you can still enjoy gourds' beauty because they're an inexpensive purchase.

Gourds grow in a full spectrum of fall colors from pale yellow to golden orange and from off-white to deep green. The colors are dramatically designed by Nature in rippling, bicolored patterns of stripes and curves. Gourds grow in a variety of shapes, for which they are often named. There are delicate pear and nest-egg gourds, yellow apple and striped-apple gourds, striped onion and mock-orange gourds, and spoon-shaped, umbrella-shaped, and crookneck gourds. One gourd is even called the Crown of Thorns or the Ten Commandments, after the ten little points that grow around its outside. The textures of gourds range from the glossy smoothness of yellow and

Gourds grow in a delightful variety of shapes and colors. A gourd-filled basket is a perfect harvest centerpiece.

striped-pear gourds to the coarse, bumpy skin of the warted gourds.

When buying gourds, look for unblemished specimens with good, consistent color. They keep their color naturally for up to six months, but if you want to preserve them longer, wipe them gently with a mixture of vinegar and water, or with a combination of any nonbleaching household detergent and water. Finish by polishing with a colorless wax—furniture or floor wax does the job. Shellac or varnish can be applied to add gloss.

Gourds are excellent for use in decorative crafts. Small gourds can be tied to a wreath to add color. They can also be strung into Charm Strings, which are made by tying several different-colored gourds together on a central, continuous string. Larger gourds can be dried out and carved into useful and decorative objects for the home. Fill them with potpourri or candy. (See page 105 for more gourd crafts.)

On Growing Gourds

Gourd plants are fairly hearty and can be grown in a garden or a plant box. They need plenty of sun and lots of moisture. If they're grown off the ground on a trellis or fence, the gourd fruits will be clean and well shaped.

Plant the seeds in the spring, after the last frost of the season. Start by making a few mounds, or little hills or earth, with six feet or so between each mound. Sow six seeds per mound. When the plants sprout, thin them out to three plants per mound. The plants take 110 to 120 days to mature.

Ornamental gourds are mature when their skin is hard and unyielding to the touch. When you're checking them don't dig your fingernails in them or the gourds will bruise. Cut the stem about an inch away from the gourd and wipe with nonbleaching disinfectant.

Gourd seeds are widely available. If, however, you can't find them at your local nursery or garden-supply store, here's a list of mail-order houses that sell gourd and other seeds:

Burpee Seed Company
Warminster, PA 18991

Gurney Seed and Nursey Company
Yankton, SD 57079

Park Seed Company
Greenwood, SC 29647

Sheaves and Dried Flowers

Wild grasses and sheaves of wheat are symbols of the harvest and Thanksgiving. The last sheaf of wheat from the year's harvest has had a special significance since ancient times. In ancient Egypt the last sheaf of wheat was offered to the goddess Mother of the Wheat. In the Middle Ages in Europe, the last sheaf was formed into a straw doll and carried in an honorary procession through the village. A more recent custom in Austria uses the last sheaf as a wreath, which crowns the head of a young girl who is named Queen of the Harvest for a day. In parts of France the last sheaf was shaped into the form of a cross and kept in the home as a token of good fortune. In Norway the last sheaf of the harvest was put outside for the birds at Christmastime, for good luck.

In late summer, take a trip to the country to gather wild flowers and grasses. Dry them carefully and use them to decorate your home for Thanksgiving.

Wheat is one of the major agricultural products of the United States. Although it isn't native to North America, it was first planted on the continent in 1607 by English colonists in Jamestown, Virginia. During the next hundred years, colonial New Jersey, Pennsylvania, and Maryland grew a surplus of wheat. As the northeastern states industrialized, settlers moved westward to start farms. Kansas, Nebraska, and Oklahoma became the three largest producers of wheat in the nation. So today, when we put a sheaf of wheat in our homes, we can regard it as a symbol of our nation's bounty and a reminder of all we have to be thankful for.

While not everyone has access to a wheat field, wild grasses and flowers grow in fields, meadows, and parks around the country. A vase or basket filled with dried grasses and wild flowers makes a perfect Thanksgiving centerpiece (see page 101). Goldenrod, milkweed, and cattails also look lovely dried. Queen Anne's lace, forsythia, oak leaves, and dogwood flowers dry well, too. Joe-pye weed, baby's breath, statice, globe amaranth, and dock all work nicely in a fall bouquet. Sprigs of bayberry and bittersweet add an extra splash of color.

When picking wild grasses and flowers, always choose dry, clean plants that are free from insects and blemishes. Never pick wet plants. Grasses and small flowers can be tied into small bunches and hung upside down from the ceiling to dry. Hang them in a warm, dark, and dry place. An attic or spare closet is just right for a drying room. Larger flowers can be preserved by dipping them carefully in a glycerin solution or a commercially available silica gel.

Indian Corn

Indian corn or maize is another symbol of bounty as well as a delightful decoration. Maize is native to both North and South America. On his explorational voyage in 1492, Christopher Columbus reported seeing maize growing in the West Indies. It played a vital role in the lives of native Americans of both continents as a staple of their diets and an element in many of their sacred myths and ceremonies.

A hidden store of Indian corn saved the Pilgrims from starvation during their first winter in Plymouth. Indian corn was also the Pilgrims' first successful crop.

Indian corn grows in white, yellow, red, purple, and variegated colors. It is used as feed for livestock and poultry, in corn oil, and in starch, corn syrup, and sugar. A few ears of Indian corn gathered in a bunch make a lovely fall decoration for the front door or entryway. For a southwestern harvest look, hang a string of dried red chili peppers (ristras), which are available at roadside stands in the southwestern states and from specialty mail-order houses (see page 155).

Wild grasses, wheat, and Indian corn are symbols of our nation's bounty.

Fun-Filled Activities and Traditions to Establish

    Thanksgiving Day provides us with many opportunities to expand old traditions and create new ones. As family and friends gather, this special day—beginning with the Macy's Thanksgiving Day Parade and culminating in a great feast—demands traditions of sharing, working together, and communal thankfulness. The activities of the day center around the preparation of Thanksgiving dinner, and, whether you are the chief cook or a member of the cleanup crew, it is this meal that unites us, reminding us of the first Thanksgiving shared by the Pilgrims and their Native American friends.

Arrange a special harvest table for your Thanksgiving guests. Cover it with a cloth, then with baskets of nuts to crack, roasted chestnuts, fruit, and other fall treats. Or, set up a table with ingredients and ask family and friends to join in the feast preparations.

The Harvest Table

For city dweller or country cousin, the richness of the holiday is splendidly represented by the earthiness and beauty of a harvest table. To enjoy the holiday most fully, work together with family and guests to prepare the table on Thanksgiving Day or the day before. Place a cloth-covered table, large enough for friends to work around, in an area far enough from the main cooking activity so as not to obstruct any work in progress. It should be laden with the bounty of the season and with harvesttime projects to busy all available hands and encourage conversation. You can reflect the spirit of the season and preparation for the winter ahead in your choices of adornments. If you live in the city, you might want to have baskets of fresh nuts ready to be shelled. To keep children's hands busy, purchase brussels sprouts, still on their stalks, from your greengrocer for children to pluck off. Chestnuts—either ready to roast or preroasted and ready to peel—are another festive addition to the harvest table (see page 32 for instructions). If your guests feel ambitious, have all the ingredients gathered for them to prepare a delicious compote that will enhance the wintry foods you'll be serving in the cold months ahead (see page 32 for recipe). The chopping and putting-up of the brandied fruit compote, roasting of nuts, and preparing the fall vegetables all add a very traditional and homespun flavor to the gathering. You will find that this extra harvest table you've set up provides the perfect opportunity for friends and family to share in the hands-on feeling of the occasion.

For those of you dwelling in suburban or country homes, what could be more in keeping with the tradition of Thanksgiving than gathering those late-season crops and roadside flowers with fellow country or city visitors? Except for those northernmost reaches of the country, hard frost will not yet have set into the garden plots, and picking chard, brussels sprouts, turnips, and jerusalem artichokes is a great, invigorating activity for a blustery—or clear—Thanksgiving Day. Additionally, these gathered, washed vegetables will add their beauty to your harvest table. Send early-arriving guests out to forage along the roadside and in woodland areas for dried flowers, beautiful branches, and pine cones, to be arranged in a basket by the front door as a seasonal welcome.

ROASTED CHESTNUTS

Here's a recipe for a seasonal favorite that will live up to what the song promises. Make a small x-shaped incision in the flat side of each nut so the nuts don't burst while cooking. Roast them in a special chestnut basket over an open fire or directly on the grillwork of an indoor gas or electric stove until dark and fragrant (about 10 minutes).

If you don't have a chestnut basket, roast the nuts in an oven on a cookie sheet at 350° for 20 to 30 minutes.

BRANDIED COMPOTE

This concoction is a welcome treat for a cold autumn day. Spooned out of a stoneware crock, compote is as delicious with cooked meats as it is ladled on ice cream. When selecting fruits, use a variety that are available in your region, including apricots, currants, prunes, figs, fresh pineapple, and frozen raspberries. Do not use apples, bananas, and grapes. Make sure the crock you use has a tight-fitting lid. Chop mixed fruit, as fresh as possible, into bite-size pieces. Combine with 1 cup sugar for each pound of fruit in a stoneware crock with a tight-fitting lid. Stir in the brandy, enough so the fruit is completely submerged, cover, and store in a cool (45° or less) spot, stirring occasionally—at least once a week. Also called Brandied Keeping Fruit, the compote will last for approximately 5 months.

Fun-Filled Activities and Traditions to Establish

A Progressive Toast

Establish a tradition of a progressive Thanksgiving toast to precede the Thanksgiving dinner. As guests arrive, whatever the time of day, have them write a few words of thankfulness and celebration—sincere, personal, or humorous—and affix these toasts to the underside of one of your other guest's plate. Before the meal begins, and once a traditional toast has been made to the occasion, have each guest at the table read the toast written by a co-celebrant.

A Thanksgiving Constitutional

The idea of a vigorous round of physical exercise on this day is an excellent one. For many of you Thanksgiving Day has become synonymous with a fiercely competitive game of football or soccer between neighboring communities. It is not too far-fetched to imagine this modern-day ritual echoing the presentation of feats of physical strength and prowess by the Indians for the Pilgrims at that first Thanksgiving. By all means encourage a neighborhood game of football, touch-football, or soccer in the afternoon before dinner. What pastime could be better to build a huge appetite for the repast to follow?

For some people low-key physical activity is a more appropriate choice of activity. Once the feast is over and the conversation has dwindled, inspire your guests to begin a traditional Thanksgiving walk, or constitutional. This is an excellent opportunity to include seldom-seen neighbors. (Let them know in advance that your gathering will be taking a walk though the neighborhood after dinner and that you would like their company, if their holiday schedule permits.) After sharing the walk with family, friends, and neighbors, invite everyone back to your home for dessert, mulled cider, cocoa, or a liqueur, and a final toast to the bounteousness, pleasure, and beauty of the day.

Macy's Parade

35

A Tradition Is Born

For many Americans, the Macy's Thanksgiving Day Parade is as much a part of the Thanksgiving celebration as turkey and pumpkin pie. Every year, nearly two million people gather along the streets of New York City to watch the floats and balloons, bands and celebrities as they make their colorful 2½-mile journey from Central Park West to Herald Square. Around the nation, more than fifty-five million people enjoy the spectacle on television from their homes.

1986 marks the parade's official sixtieth anniversary. This American tradition actually began in 1924 when a group of Macy's employees, many of them first-generation immigrants from Europe, wanted to create a celebration like the harvest festivals they remembered from their native lands. So they planned a big Thanksgiving Day parade to welcome in the holiday season.

The first parade was a big event in New York. Traveling a long route, from 145th Street and Convent Avenue in

Harlem, all the way down to 34th Street at Herald Square, it featured Macy's employees dressed as clowns, giants, cowboys and cowgirls, knights in armor, and sheiks. There were floats and bands, and even live lions, tigers, and bears from the Central Park Zoo. The parade was so well received by New Yorkers that Macy's decided to turn it into an annual tradition. And they did.

The parade has assembled and marched every year since 1924, except for the years 1942 to 1944, when the United States was fighting in World War II. In 1942 the parade made its own contribution to the war effort. The huge parade balloons were donated to New York's Mayor Fiorello La Guardia on the steps of city hall; he gave them, in turn, to the Armed Forces who used the 650-pound present for scrap rubber, which was badly needed.

In 1945 the war was over and the Macy's parade started up again, better than ever. That year, it was televised locally for the first time. Three years later, in 1948, NBC broadcast it nationally, and in 1960, to the delight of all those Americans with color televisions, it was telecast in color.

Because of its enormous television audience, the quality of the parade broadcast is almost as important as the quality of the parade itself. Working together, Macy's and NBC provide award-winning entertainment for their viewers. Their hard work has been rewarded with more than just audience enjoyment. In 1979, 1982, and 1983, the parade broadcast won Emmies for outstanding achievement in the production of special events and technical direction.

In 1924, a group of Macy's employees planned a Thanksgiving Day Parade to welcome the holiday season. It was very successful, instantly on its way to becoming an American tradition.

HOTEL
ASTOR
LOEWS STATE
Pepsi-Cola
HOTEL CLARIDGE
Camel
WPIX
CHIN'S
NEWMAN'S THEATRE TICKETS

A Tradition Is Born

Early parades featured live animals, balloons and floats, and Macy's employees dressed in fantastic costumes. At the end of the parade all the balloons, large and small, were released in a marvelous flurry.

39

Planning the Parade

Planning the parade is a complex, year-round process that involves designing new floats and balloons and restoring and updating old ones, auditioning and selecting marching bands, staging and coordinating celebrities, and creating new themes and costumes for the Macy's employees who participate in the parade.

Macy's Special Productions Department organizes the parade each year. The Parade Director and a team of dedicated managers orchestrate the whole parade, working with a committee of thirty Macy's employees from all different departments within the store. The committee is responsible for selecting several "captains" for each parade job. The captains, in turn, recruit individual Macy's employees who want to be part of the parade. During the four weekends before Thanksgiving, workshops are held for over two thousand parade participants, to teach them balloon handling, clowning, float escorting, and other parade arts. If you can, watch the 1947 movie *A Miracle on 34th Street* for the funny parade-planning scene that introduces the film's wonderful Santa.

Floats are built in Macy's own studio in Hoboken, New Jersey, right across the river from Manhattan. The floats are designed to look as authentic as possible.

A Tradition Is Born

The parade begins at Seventy-seventh Street and Central Park West, and proceeds along the park to Broadway. Here, the parade reaches its finale at Macy's, at Thirty-fourth Street and Seventh Avenue.

The Parade Route

The parade begins at Seventy-seventh Street and Central Park West, near the American Museum of Natural History, and proceeds south, along the tree-lined border of Central Park, past the historic buildings of Manhattan's Upper West Side. Noteworthy buildings along Central Park West include the New-York Historical Society, founded in 1804; the Dakota, completed in 1884, the famous apartment building where the late John Lennon, a former Beatle, lived with his family; and the Majestic Apartments, built in the thirties in the Art Deco style.

At the end of Central Park West, the parade passes by the modern forty-four-story Gulf and Western Building, by the New York Coliseum, and through Columbus Circle, where it crosses over to Broadway. In the center of Columbus Circle is a statue of Christopher Columbus, erected in 1894.

The parade continues down Broadway, through the world-famous theater district, by Times Square with its flashing neon signs, then into the "canyons" of Broadway from Fortieth Street to Herald Square. The tall office buildings that line both sides of the street house New York City's garment district. The parade concludes in front of Macy's on Thirty-fourth Street.

41

Macy's Thanksgiving Book

Macy's giant balloons and floats delight children and spectators of all ages.

The Best Viewing Spots

Where's the best place to watch the parade? The answer depends on how much time you want to spend watching it.

If you want the short version, set up near the starting line at Seventy-seventh Street and Central Park West. When the parade starts, it moves smoothly and fairly quickly. You can see the whole procession go by, from beginning to end, in about an hour and a half. For a longer version, stand along Broadway, below Columbus Circle. According to the Macy's parade staff, the parade slows down at Columbus Circle, when it switches over from Central Park West to Broadway. Count on three hours for viewing the whole parade from Broadway.

There are no seats available for the public, so make sure you're wearing comfortable shoes. You'll be standing or walking for a long time. It's a good idea to check the weather the morning of the parade. Remember to bring plenty of warm clothes, or an umbrella, if necessary.

If you're coming from out of town and want to treat yourself and your family, book a hotel room with a view of the parade route. You can watch the parade out your window and enjoy close-ups of the floats, balloons, bands, and celebrities on television.

New York has a limited number of hotel rooms with good parade views. Try the Marriot Marquis, the Mayflower, the Novotel, or the smaller Westpark. Make sure to book your room several months in advance. The Mayflower recommends reserving the room up to a year before the parade, and the Marriot Marquis suggests six to eight months. Request a room with a view of either Central Park West or Broadway. (For more information on New York hotels, contact the New York Convention and Visitors Bureau at 212-397-8222.)

Many offices along Broadway and Central Park West open up so their employees can enjoy the parade from indoors. Ask friends who work in New York City if they have access to a good viewing spot.

A Tradition Is Born

Macy's Thanksgiving Book

Preparations for the parade begin at 6:00 P.M. Thanksgiving eve and continue through the night. The balloons are inflated, the floats are assembled, and the bands rehearse their performance.

Tips for Spectators

At 6:00 P.M. on Thanksgiving eve, preparations for the parade begin, and they continue through the night. Many New Yorkers and parade fans from out of town enjoy watching the preparations. The preparade activities take place at two locations: the start and finish of the parade route. They are open to the general public.

First, you can watch the balloons come to life at Seventy-seventh Street between Central Park West and Columbus Avenue, right next to the American Museum of Natural History. At 7:00 P.M., the deflated balloons arrive at the starting line, and there they are transformed from shapeless masses of nylon into enormous storybook and cartoon characters. At 11:00 P.M. the balloons are just beginning to come to life.

If you wait long enough, you can watch the floats being assembled. At 1:00 A.M., the float convoy passes through Lincoln Tunnel carrying the floats, which have been broken up into components for transport. It proceeds to the Seventy-seventh-Street site where the Macy's float-assembly crew works all night, putting the floats back together.

At Herald Square — Thirty-fourth Street and Broadway — in the wee hours of the morning, the bands practice their Herald Square performances for the television cameras before they head uptown for the start of the parade. The public is welcome to enjoy the parade preview at Herald Square, too.

44

A Tradition Is Born

Balloons

Generations of children have thrilled to the sight of their favorite storybook characters floating down Broadway, larger than life. Over the years, the Macy's parade has brought to life such favorites as Mickey Mouse and Donald Duck, Bullwinkle the Moose, Underdog, Snoopy, and Elsie the Cow. Fans in the 1980s have enjoyed the sight of Kermit the frog, Woody Woodpecker, Garfield the cat, Superman, and Betty Boop, who is perched coyly on a crescent moon.

Each year a few new balloons are introduced to the parade and old ones are retired. Creating a new balloon involves several steps. First, the Macy's balloon designers made a blueprint of the new balloon, using stuffed animals, toys, and other models as their guide. After a prototype is built and approved by the Macy's staff and designers, it's time to start constructing the real thing.

The balloons are made in several different sections. Each section is sealed separately so that if one part of the

Underdog floats by Macy's Department Store in 1977 (left), and Bullwinkle towers over the Centerville Ohio High School Band in 1982 (above).

Macy's Thanksgiving Book

balloon, such as an arm or a leg, hits an obstacle, the rest of the balloon remains intact. Each of the balloon's sections is cut individually from huge lengths of urethane-coated nylon. An enormous amount of material is used. For example, 565 square yards of material were used for Raggedy Ann's floral-patterned dress and white pinafore, red-and-white socks, and black shoes. Olive Oyl's hands alone are eight feet and eight inches long from wrist to fingertips! Yogi Bear used 400 yards of nylon and 30 gallons of light brown, green, and white paint to come to life.

After each section of the balloon is cut and sealed, all the individual chambers are sealed together to create the finished product. Then balloons are handpainted according to the original blueprints and color renderings. Details such as eyes, noses, freckles, and smiles are painted on by talented artists. The building and refurbishing of balloons goes on throughout the year.

At 7:00 P.M. on Thanksgiving eve, the deflated balloons arrive at the parade starting line at Seventy-seventh Street, right next to the American Museum of Natural History. The streets have already been cleared and covered with drop cloths. First, the balloons are unrolled from their tarps onto drop cloths and laid out lengthwise along the street. When they are lying deflated on the street, they look like masses of shiny plastic bags.

Once they are all carefully set out, Macy's balloon technicians inflate them with a mixture of helium and air, pumped from gleaming white tank trucks, while delighted spectators watch them come to life.

Every year hundreds of people come to watch the balloons being blown up. Rain or shine, the balloon fans are out there, walking up and down the block, stopping to look at their favorite balloon or to watch as another one takes form. Among the spectators are tourists from all over the country who have come to visit family or friends and watch the parade; and some New Yorkers come every year to see the balloon inflation. Some favorite balloons of the younger fans are Snoopy, Garfield, Raggedy Ann, and Woody Woodpecker.

It takes a lot of the helium-and-air mixture to fill the balloons. The average balloon is five to six stories high when fully inflated. Garfield, the huge orange cat, is 60 feet high and 35 feet wide and requires 18,907 cubic feet of helium. Superman, the largest balloon every built for the Macy's parade, needs 14,000 cubic feet of

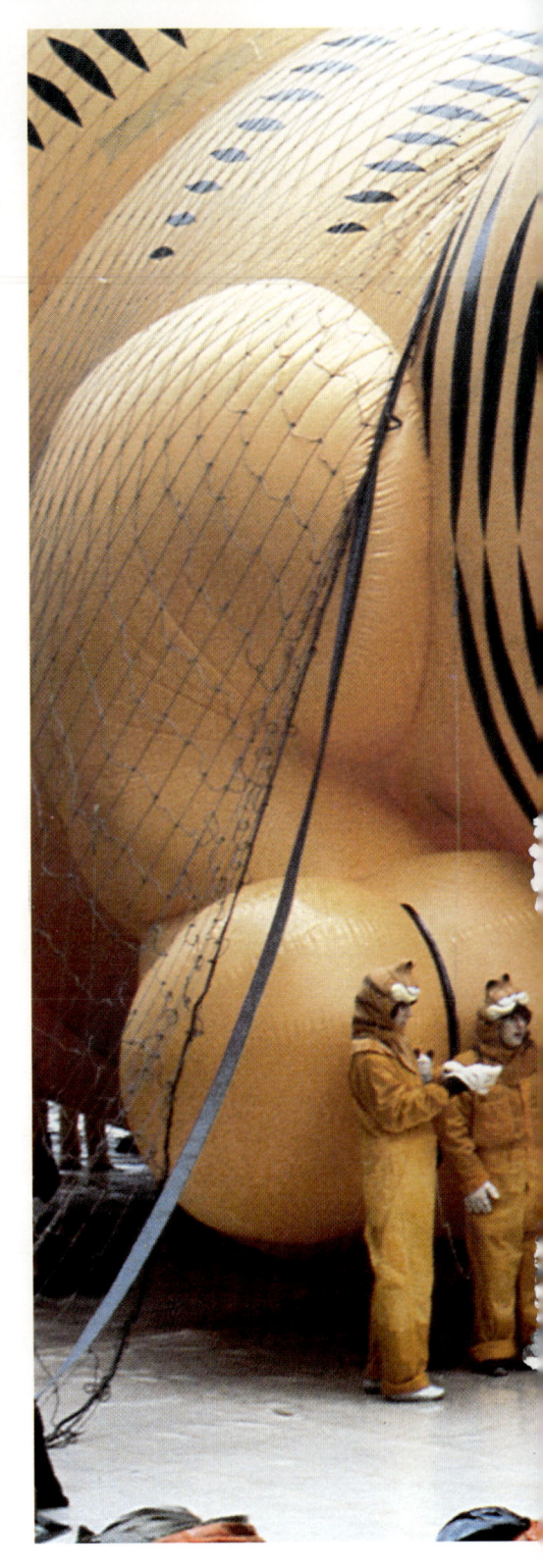

The average balloon is six stories high. Yogi Bear required 400 yards of nylon and 30 gallons of paint to come to life. It took 565 square yards of material to make Raggedy Ann's dress, socks, and shoes.

48

Balloons

The night before the parade, the balloons are inflated with a mixture of helium and air. Because they are so large, the balloons require a huge quantity of this mixture. For example, Garfield the cat needs 18,907 cubic feet of helium.

Macy's Thanksgiving Book

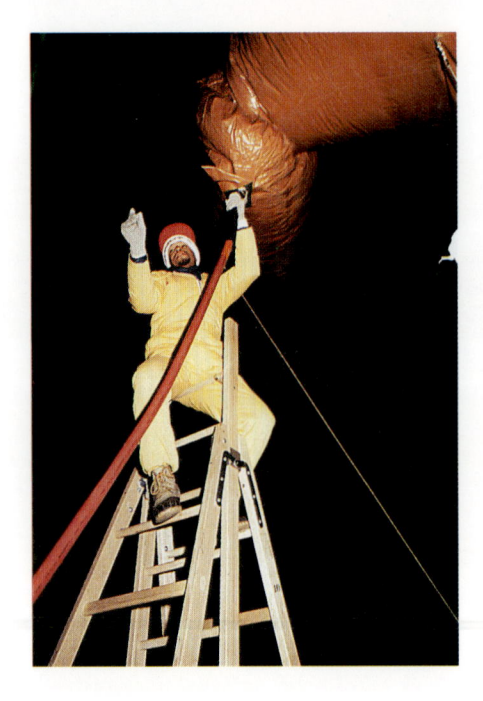

The helium-and-air mixture is pumped from tank trucks into the balloons.

Enthusiastic balloon handlers are outfitted to match their favorite balloon.

The details on each balloon are still hand-painted by talented artists. Here, in 1934, Mickey Mouse is getting his famous smile.

This balloon is in the final stages of inflation. Notice the size of its hand.

50

Balloons

Macy's Thanksgiving Book

Kermit the Frog (left) and Superman (see page 51) are two of the parade fans' favorites. Kermit was invited to England in 1979, where he soared over London's Hyde Park—even Queen Elizabeth came to see him. This is the first in the series of Superman balloons. He made his premier appearance in Macy's 1940 parade.

The parade's first balloons were designed by Tony Sarg, the theatrical designer and creator of Macy's Christmas windows. The dragon (below) is one of the first balloons.

the helium mixture in his 14 separate compartments. When fully inflated, he is 104 feet long, 35 feet wide, and weighs 550 pounds.

By Thanksgiving morning all the balloons are ready for the parade. But they can't make the voyage downtown by themselves. Macy's employees who have been trained to handle the balloons in all kinds of weather hold each balloon by long strings. Depending on their size and weight, balloons need from twenty to forty handlers to be kept under control.

The balloon handlers are costumed according to the balloon's character or theme. For example, Garfield's handlers wear "Garfield gold" coveralls and a specially molded cat headpiece with handpainted stripes. Raggedy Ann's handlers dress as her best friend, Raggedy Andy. Kermit's twenty-five handlers wear costumes of frog green.

The Kermit balloon has become an international celebrity. In 1979 it was invited to England to celebrate the International Year of the Child. Soaring in the air over London's Hyde Park, Kermit entertained Queen Elizabeth II and thousands of English children.

In 1985 a new visual level was introduced to the parade with Macy's flying balloon scenes, such as Betty Boop cradled in a crescent moon. Another new element was the ten-foot-diameter "ornamental balloons." Decorated with Thanksgiving and Christmas motifs, they are carried by groups of clowns.

Balloons were first introduced to the parade in 1927. Before then, live lions, tigers, and bears rode the floats. But these live animals growled and roared as they passed by, frightening many young spectators. So in 1927 Tony Sarg, the theatrical designer and creator of Macy's Christmas windows, was asked to design rubber animal balloons to replace live animals. The first balloons were Felix the Cat, a dragon, an elephant, and a toy soldier. The big balloons seemed friendly to young viewers, who liked them much better than the scary live animals.

In 1928 the giant character balloons and thousands of smaller balloons were released in front of Macy's at the end of the parade. They shot straight up in the air and exploded! None of the people in charge of the parade remembered that helium expands at high altitudes, causing an explosion.

So in 1929 safety valves were added to the balloons to keep them from bursting. That year, they were sent up again after the parade. Attached to each balloon was a label with a return address and an offer of a prize to whoever found them. One year, a dachshund balloon landed in the East River. Two tugboats raced for the prize and tore the balloon apart in their eagerness to retrieve it. Another year, Andy the Alligator split into two parts, and the two people who found it had to share the reward.

In the early thirties, daring aviators chased the giant balloons from their airplanes and either successfully caught or collided with them. One story tells of a student pilot who was practicing her flying skills over Jamaica Bay (near New York City) when, suddenly, she saw the giant cat balloon floating through the sky. To the dismay of her instructor, she headed straight for the balloon and collided with it. Fortunately, although the collision stalled her engine, she managed to regain control. Another story tells of the famous aviator, Clarence Chamberlin, who hooked a pig balloon with a tow rope and brought it down to earth over Prospect Park in Brooklyn. Because of these and other dangerous exploits, Macy's had to discontinue the practice of releasing the big balloons after the parade.

To keep the parade audience from feeling any disappointment, Macy's came up with an entirely new idea: The balloons were given sound effects. In 1933 the crying-baby balloon cried, Andy the Alligator hissed, the dachshund barked, and the pig oinked. The following year, Tony Sarg collaborated with Walt Disney on balloon designs and Mickey Mouse, Horace Horse Collar, and the Big Bad Wolf were introduced.

Through the years, the balloons have suffered some major and minor mishaps. In 1941 the Santa Claus balloon burst while it was being inflated. In 1956 Gobbler the Turkey and a Civil War balloon were knocked out by forty-five-mile-an-hour winds. But Mickey Mouse managed to make it to the finish line, where he finally collapsed. The following year, Popeye collected gallons of rain in his fourteen-foot hat, which set him teetering off balance. In 1958 there was a helium shortage, which forced Macy's to fill the balloons with air and carry them down the parade route, hoisted aloft on cranes. In 1975 a strong gust of wind sent Underdog crashing into a streetlight in Times Square. Due to heavy wind and rain in 1985 Kermit rode so low to the ground that he looked as if he were swimming, which is quite appropriate for a frog! But no matter what the weather conditions, Macy's balloon handlers always do their best to bring the balloons to the finish line. And spectators are always there to appreciate their efforts!

In 1932, the crocodile balloon was released at the parade's finish line at Thirty-fourth Street. This practice took place from 1927-1933. (Note the Sixth Avenue elevated subway, which was torn down in 1939.)

Many favorites, such as Smokey the Bear, appear for several years in a row.

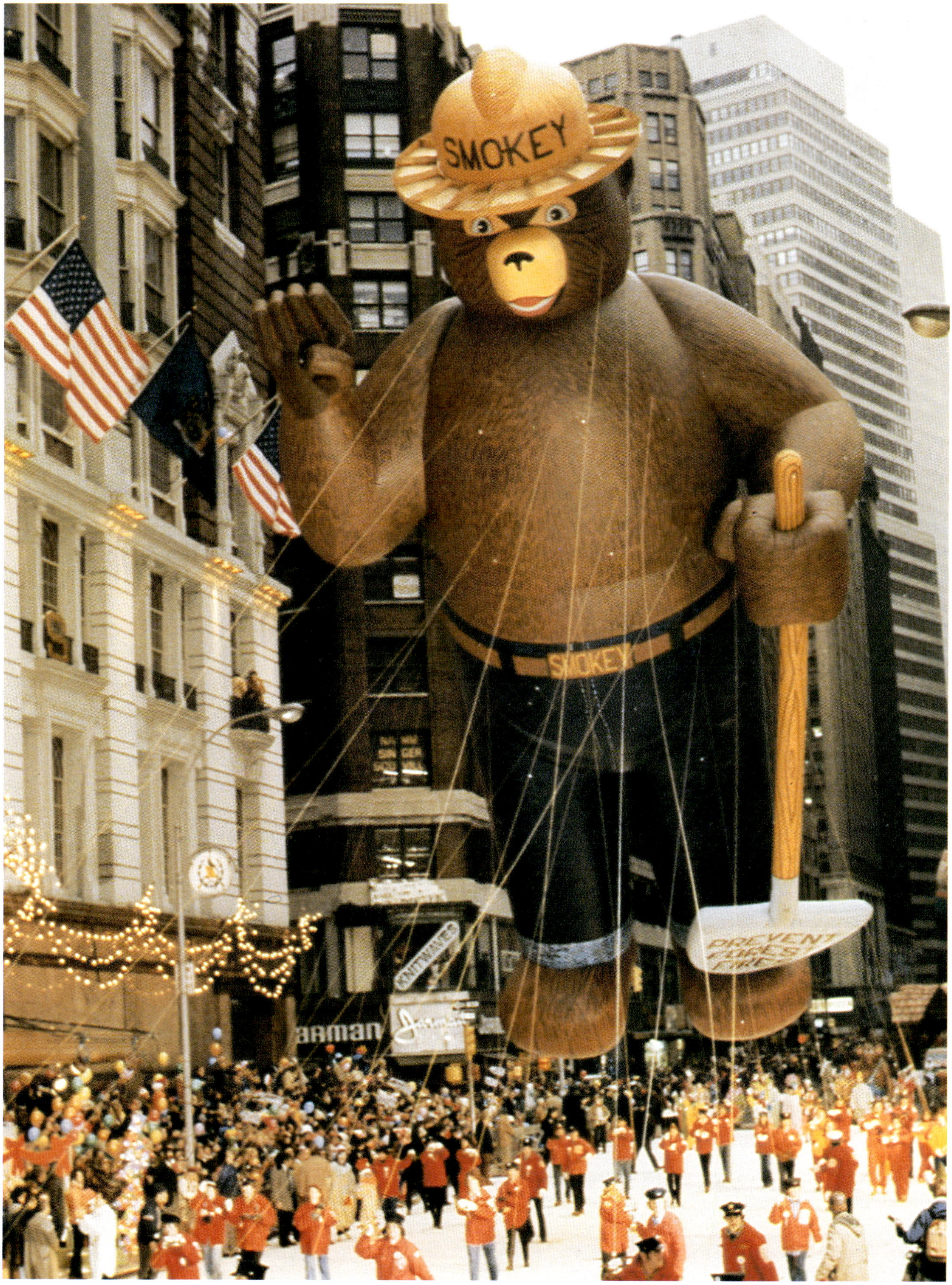
SMOKEY
SMOKEY
PREVENT FOREST FIRE
KNITWAVES

Floats, Celebrities, and Bands

Floats

Floats bring life and color to the Macy's parade, and bands and celebrities add music and laughter. Every year, there are sixteen to eighteen floats in the parade, twelve bands, and many celebrities, performers, and dance troupes. Each float carries several Macy's employees who are dressed in elaborate costumes to match the theme of the float.

Floats have been part of the parade since the very beginning. In 1925 a Santa Claus float was accompanied by twenty-five women, all Macy's employees, dressed as Snow Babies in fur-trimmed parkas. The 1955 parade featured the world's largest birthday cake on the Birthday in Tootsieland float, topped by a huge candle that resembled a giant Tootsie Roll. The candle emitted a real flame, powered by an acetylene torch.

Macy's builds a few new floats each year, to the delight of the parade audience. The parades of the 1980s have featured the Cabbage Patch Kids float, the Rainbow Brite float, the Care Bears float, the Masters of the Uni-

Macy's employees wear colorful costumes that complement the floats.

verse, The Statue of Liberty, and the Disneyland Celebration floats, to name a few.

Let's take a close look at one of the parade favorites: the Care Bears float. This float carries ten performers dressed as the ten Care Bears: Bedtime Bear, Birthday Bear, Cheer Bear, Friend Bear, Funshine Bear, Good Luck Bear, Grumpy Bear, Love-A-Lot Bear, Tenderheart Bear, and Wish Bear. The float is built on two separate float beds that are bridged by a huge steel-and-wood rainbow and surrounded by fluffy fiberglass clouds. A five-story turreted castle sits at the end of the rainbow. Bedtime Bear is rocked to sleep on a twelve-foot crescent moon, suspended from the clouds. Eighteen Macy's employees dressed as giant multicolored hearts escort the colorful float. Care Bears is just one example of the many spectacular floats Macy's has designed over the years.

The average lifetime of a float is two to three years, but some favorites just keep coming back. The Doodlebug, for example, with its long eyelashes and its big blue eyes, has been in the parade for more than ten years. It used to be green, but it was recently repainted yellow. The Santa Claus and turkey floats are classic favorites that are frequently redecorated and refurbished to please each new generation of young audiences.

All the floats are built by Macy's in a former candy factory in Hoboken, New Jersey, just across the river from New York City. Before the floats can be built, a good deal of preliminary discussion, research, and design goes on. Macy's Parade Designer and his construction crew create new float ideas, aiming for authenticity and constructing the floats so they look as realistic as possible.

Here's a fun bit of Macy's parade lore. Many years ago, a Noah's Ark float was being built in the float studio in Hoboken, and it started to rain. It rained continually, as it sometimes does in the New York area, for two weeks in a row. The studio's landlord was worried about flooding in the building, so he stopped by the studio to have a look. Imagine how much more concerned he became when he saw a giant ark under construction.

Float designers work with a detailed production schedule. All float designs must be completed by the February before the next Thanksgiving, to leave plenty of time for construction and painting.

The Macy's floats are built of papier

The Doodlebug float is a real veteran, having been in the parade for ten years. The bright yellow float with long eyelashes carries a special passenger, Paddington Bear.

Macy's Thanksgiving Book

Before a float is built, designers create a miniature model of it. This is a model of the Robotman & Friends™ float.

The life-size Robotman & Friends under construction at the parade studio.

mâché, and coated with fiberglass to protect them from the elements. When the floats are completed, most stand more than 40 feet high, but they are modular; they are built to be folded into 8- by 12½-foot components so they can pass through the Lincoln Tunnel on their way to and from the parade.

At 1 A.M. on Thanksgiving Day, one tube of the Lincoln Tunnel is closed, so the float convoy can proceed to the starting line. The floats are folded up into their small components for transport. Macy's crews work through the night, reassembling the floats, and putting on the final touches before their ride down the parade route.

At 9 A.M. the parade kicks off and the colorful floats travel down the parade route accompanied by singing celebrities, actors, and dancers who perform for the cheering crowds. The big floats are interspersed with balloons, marching bands, bevies of clowns, and the smaller "push" floats and "rocking animal" floats.

The push floats are pushed or pulled by costumed Macy's employees. Some traditional favorites include the Pilgrim man and woman with their Indian friend escorts, President George Washington, and statesman Ben Franklin.

Then there's the whole family of rocking animal floats: the rocking turtle, rocking lion, and several others accompanied by escorts in matching costumes. The rocking floats are brightly painted creatures that sit on large rockers, like old-fashioned rocking horses. Famous singers sit astride them and sing their hit songs as they pass by. Some floats re-

58

Floats, Celebrities, and Bands

ceive particularly special attention: The rocking lobster is accompanied by forty old-fashioned bathing beauties; Mrs. Rocking Kangaroo comes with her eight baby 'roos; and the giant white rocking horse, a veteran of many Macy's Thanksgiving Day parades, is escorted by a group of living toys.

When the Santa Claus float pulls up in front of Macy's, the parade is just about over. Accompanied by reindeer and riding his sleigh, Santa Claus signals the end of the parade and the beginning of the Christmas season.

Celebrities

Celebrities add a special, glamorous spark to the parade. Viewers enjoy the sight of familiar faces as they ride by on the floats. There are stars from each year's favorite television shows and from current Broadway plays. There are country singers, pop singers, opera singers, comedians, and of course, the high-stepping Rockettes.

The marquee at Herald Square is the stage for celebrity performances. In front of Macy's, famous actors perform scenes from Broadway plays, the Rockettes dance, and celebrities sing from atop the floats. There are talented jugglers, cavorting clowns, acrobats, gymnasts, and mimes. No matter what the weather, thousands of spectators gather around to watch the show. On rainy parade days, myriad umbrellas add color to the scene.

When it comes to choosing celebrities to perform in the parade, there is no lack of available talent. Many performers grew up watching the parade every year and feel honored to be part of it. Some singers and performers enjoy the publicity it brings them, while others do it just for the fun of it.

Through the years, many world-famous celebrities have been part of the parade. Both Harpo Marx and Benny Goodman performed at the marquee. The 1947 parade featured Maureen O'Hara and John Payne, the stars of the award-winning movie, *Miracle on 34th Street*. In 1953 Sid Caesar, Imogene Coca, and Steve Allen performed. Celeste Holm dressed up as Little Bo Peep and Eddie Fisher wore the royal garb of Prince Charming. In 1955 Danny Kaye was Grand Marshal of the parade, and in 1958 the Rockettes made their first appearance along with Ginger Rogers, Charlie Ruggles, and Dick Clark. In 1960 Bob Hope was King of the Parade.

Recent parades have included pop-singer and actress Irene Cara, comedian

Floats, Celebrities, and Bands

Celebrities add to the glamour of the parade. Spectators have been entertained by such favorites as (clockwise from top left) *Fred Flintstone, Jackie Gleason, posing here with Santa Claus, TV show host, Ed McMahon, numerous clowns, magicians, and jugglers, the world-famous Rockettes, and the talented entertainer, Ann Miller.*

61

Macy's Thanksgiving Book

The music of marching bands keeps the parade moving along. Macy's selects the best twelve out of hundreds of bands who apply to play in the parade. These bands come from all over the United States. Shown here is the Winchester Community High School Band from Winchester, Indiana.

The Colquitt County High School Band is from Moultrie, Georgia.

The U.S. Marines Drum and Bugle Corps (left) from Washington, D.C., put on a spectacular performance in front of Macy's. The band finale at the parade's finish line (right) makes a colorful scene.

62

Floats, Celebrities, and Bands

Dom Deluise, opera star Placido Domingo, and singer Dionne Warwick, to name a few.

Bands

The music of the marching bands keeps the parade moving along. High school bands come to New York from all over the country, Canada, the Virgin Islands, Puerto Rico, and even England, to play in the parade.

Every year, Macy's receives three hundred applications from many high school and a few college bands. The bands send in videotapes, photographs, and cassettes of their performances. They are judged not only for their musical ability but also for their costumes, their marching ability, and the skills of their other performances as well. During the parade, they have to provide both music and entertainment.

Macy's Parade Staff selects several possible bands from the three hundred applications. Then they send out talent scouts to watch the bands perform in their hometowns. Finally, they narrow their selection down to the twelve best. But the Macy's staff makes sure to select bands from different states every year.

The band members pay for their own trips to New York. Some have special fund-raisers to earn the necessary money. Many band members bring their families, and Macy's sets up a special grandstand at the parade's starting line for the bands' families and chaperones.

From 3:30 to 6:00 A.M. on the day of the parade, the bands rehearse their Herald Square performances in front of the television cameras. At 9:00 A.M. they're at the starting line, ready to go. They play their way down the parade route to Herald Square, providing music and rhythm for the other parade performers. At the finish line, each band presents something special. It could be a performance by flag teams, dancers, baton twirlers, or rifle corps. The music they play ranges from the latest pop tunes to joyful classical pieces. When their performances are over, the bands receive a resounding round of applause, and thus another parade heralds in the holiday season.

The Celebration

65

A Traditional Thanksgiving Meal

~~~~~

When most families sit down to the Thanksgiving feast, they prepare a meal similar to the one that follows. Stuffing, vegetable, and potato techniques vary between regions and family tradition, but the pies will almost always be pumpkin, the relish cranberry, the potatoes whipped, and the turkey bursting with richness. The biggest constant is overeating—and the sandwiches that follow recovery.

ROAST TURKEY AND GRAVY

Turkey:
15- to 20-pound turkey
16 tablespoons butter

Gravy:
Neck and giblets
Medium onion
Large carrot
3 bay leaves
½–¾ cup white wine
Salt to taste
Pepper to taste
2 tablespoons flour

Turkey: Preheat the oven to 350°. Fill a 15- to 20-pound turkey with the currant stuffing, spooning it in both the neck and stomach cavities. Close the cavity with string or larding needle. Soak a piece of cheesecloth in lukewarm melted butter. Place the turkey on an interior rack of a lidded roasting pan, cover the breast and thighs with cheesecloth. Place in oven, covered. Baste at 45-minute intervals. The turkey should take at least 2½ to 3½ hours, depending on the size and preferred doneness of the bird.

After the turkey has been in for 2 to 3 hours, remove lid and cheesecloth and allow to brown, basting at intervals with the pan juices. The thigh joint should be about 145° when the turkey is done, with the juices running clear but still slightly tinged with pink. Allow the turkey to rest 10 to 15 minutes before carving.

Gravy: While the turkey roasts, start a small stock with the neck, giblets, onion, carrot, bay leaves, and ½ cup white wine. Add a small amount of water. When the stock has simmered for a while and the carrot is tender, strain it and season with salt and pepper. Begin to reduce it slowly (see box on Deglazing).

Pour off most of the fat from the roasting pan and deglaze the brown juices with more white wine. Pour this into the strained, reduced stock; adjust seasonings for salt, pepper, and more wine and reduce. Mix together the flour and ½ cup of very cold water. Add this mixture gradually to the gravy; you'll probably only use about half of the mixture.

Deglazing

Deglazing is the term used to describe the first step of preparing a sauce or gravy from pan juices—those from roasted or even sauteed poultry or meat. Most of the fat is carefully poured from the pan and any juices or brown material saved. The pan is then placed on the stove, wine or water is added, and the pan is heated while the bottom is scraped carefully to free any flavorful bits that may be stuck there. In the process of the heating and scraping—the deglazing—the wine or water begins to cook down, the mixture thickens, and a sauce is born and ready to be seasoned, thickened, and served.

CURRANT STUFFING

2 to 3 large bermuda onions
1½ tablespoons butter
8 cups dried, unseasoned bread cubes
1½ cups currants
1 cup walnut meats
2 teaspoons sage
Salt
Pepper

Sauté the onions in the butter until tender, then blend into other ingredients. Season to taste and fill the turkey's stomach and throat cavities. The remainder can be placed in a 375° oven and crisped for 15 minutes before the turkey is ready to come out of the oven, then mixed with the stuffing from the cavity and baked for another 15 minutes.

Timetable for Roasting Fresh or Thawed Turkey or Turkey Parts

WEIGHT (POUNDS)	UNSTUFFED (HOURS)	STUFFED (HOURS)
4 to 6 (breasts)	1 1/2 to 2 1/4	Not applicable
6 to 8	2 1/4 to 3 1/4	3 to 3 1/2
8 to 12	3 to 4	3 1/2 to 4 1/2
12 to 16	3 1/2 to 4 1/2	4 1/2 to 5 1/2
16 to 20	4 to 5	5 1/2 to 6 1/2
20 to 24	4 1/2 to 5 1/2	6 1/2 to 7
24 to 28	5 to 6 1/2	7 to 8 1/2
Drumsticks, quarters, thighs	2 to 3 1/2	Not applicable

Source: Laura Fox, U.S. Dep't. of Agriculture, Home and Garden Bulletin No. 243

CREAMED BABY LEEKS AND PEARL ONIONS

20 pearl onions
10 small leeks
3 tablespoons butter
3 tablespoons flour
1 1/2 cups milk
1/2 cup grated Vermont cheddar
Salt to taste
Pepper to taste

Trim onions, and trim and wash leeks carefully. Dry and sauté briefly (2 to 3 minutes). Layer in a small, buttered baking dish. Set aside.

Melt butter in a heavy, preferably enameled, saucepan over low heat. Add flour and stir for 2 to 3 minutes, raising the flame slightly. Add cold milk and whisk out any lumps. Stir constantly until the béchamel thickens. Add cheddar, stir until melted, and remove from flame. Season liberally with salt and pepper. Cover the onions and leeks with the béchamel sauce, and bake in a 350° oven for 30 minutes.

FRESH CRANBERRY RELISH

1 pound whole, fresh cranberries
2 oranges, zested and juiced
1 lemon, zested and juiced
1 cup white sugar
2 tablespoons bourbon

Mix all ingredients and simmer in a saucepan until the cranberries begin to pop their skins and soften, about 10 to 15 minutes. Do not allow them to overcook and become mushy. Chill in jars in the refrigerator or can and preserve the relish for later use.

WILD RICE WITH CHANTERELLES AND FRESH CHIVES

3 1/2 cups water
2 cups wild rice, rinsed
2 cups fresh chanterelles or 3/4 cup dried
2 shallots, finely chopped
6 tablespoons butter
6 tablespoons chives or 4 tablespoons scallions, finely chopped
Freshly ground black pepper
Salt

If using dried chanterelles, place in a bowl, add a pinch of salt, and barely cover with boiling water. Let them sit 3 hours, or until adequately softened. Dry carefully.

Salt water and bring to a boil in a heavy saucepan. Add rice and simmer, stirring occasionally, for 20 to 30 minutes, until rice is tender but still has a bite. Drain excess water and set aside.

Clean fresh chanterelles with a moistened cloth, not under water. Slice fresh or dried chanterelles to a 1/3-inch width. Sauté with the shallots in 4 tablespoons of butter over medium heat for about 7 minutes and stir into the rice. Add the chives, pepper, and the remaining butter. Serve immediately.

Turkey Tips

- Figure on one pound of turkey per person. This will provide enough for leftovers the next day.
- The younger the turkey, the more tender and mild flavored it will be.
- Store a fresh turkey at 40° or below, and use it within one to two days.
- If you're freezing fresh turkey parts, wrap them in freezer paper or heavy-duty aluminum foil, store them at 0° or below, and use them within five or six months.
- If you have a frozen, prestuffed turkey, do *not* thaw it before cooking; the stuffing can attract harmful bacteria.
- Wash your hands, utensils, and sink after they have come in contact with raw turkey. This will help prevent the spread of bacteria.
- Stuff a turkey at the last minute. Allow three-quarters of a cup of stuffing for every pound of ready-to-cook turkey. Extra stuffing may be baked separately.
- Use a meat thermometer for accuracy. Insert it into the thickest part of the thigh muscle without touching the bone. This area heats most slowly.
- To brown a turkey, place a foil tent on the bird until 20 to 30 minutes before the roasting is done. Remove the foil and continue cooking until the thermometer registers 185°.
- Have any questions? Call or write to the Meat and Poultry Hotline, USDA, FSIS, Room 1163-S, Washington, DC 20250, (202) 472-4485. (Do not call collect.)

Source: Adapted from Laura Fox, U.S. Dep't. of Agriculture, Home and Garden Bulletin No. 243

A Traditional Thanksgiving Meal

Macy's Thanksgiving Book

LETTUCE SALAD WITH GRAPEFRUIT

Lettuce Salad:
1 head red leaf lettuce
1 head green leaf lettuce
1 small red onion, thinly sliced
1 small pink grapefruit, sectioned

Simple Vinaigrette:
1/4 cup tarragon or champagne vinegar
1/2 teaspoon dry mustard
1/4 teaspoon salt
1/8 teaspoon sugar
2/3 cup extra-virgin olive oil
1 crushed garlic clove

Lettuce Salad: Wash, dry, and rip lettuce, keeping the leaves fairly large. Arrange in the salad bowl and top with red onion. Peel the grapefruit sections of white pulp and rip in half if they are large.

Simple Vinaigrette: Blend the vinegar and seasonings; whisk in the oil. Let the garlic clove rest in the vinaigrette for an hour before dressing the salad.

GARLIC POTATOES

1 head garlic
8 to 12 tablespoons butter
6 large Idaho potatoes
1 small rutabaga (enough for 2 cups), mashed
1/3 to 1/2 cup heavy cream (as needed)
Freshly ground black pepper to taste
Salt to taste

Peel the garlic cloves and poach slowly in the butter using a small, covered saucepan. When soft—approximately 30 minutes—mash them into the butter.

Peel the potatoes and rutabaga, and cut them into 2-inch-by-1-inch pieces. In separate pans boil each until tender. Mash the rutabaga and place in a large bowl; mash the potatoes with the heavy cream and add the mixture to the rutabaga, along with the garlic-butter mixture. Mix until smooth and fine in texture.

Season, place in a buttered baking dish, and bake at 375° until the top browns. Serve immediately.

BROCCOLI PUREE

3 pounds broccoli
8 tablespoons butter
1 tablespoon grated onion
1 egg, beaten
3 tablespoons heavy cream
1 teaspoon freshly ground black pepper
Pinch of salt
1 teaspoon freshly grated nutmeg
1/3 cup grated parmesan (preferably reggiano)

Cut the broccoli stalks from the florets and slice into small (1-inch) pieces. Bring a pot of salted water to a boil, add the stalks, and cook for 5 minutes. Add the florets and cook for an additional 4 minutes or until all pieces are tender but still firm. Drain well and puree in a food processor or blender.

Remove to a mixing bowl and add 7 tablespoons of melted butter, grated onion, egg, cream, pepper, salt, and nutmeg. Blend thoroughly, adjust seasonings, and fold in half of the parmesan.

Lightly butter a 2-quart baking dish with the remaining tablespoon of butter. Top with remaining parmesan and bake in a preheated 375° oven for 15 minutes or until the cheese is golden and the puree is warm in the center.

Thawing a Turkey in the Refrigerator

Use the chart that follows. Place the turkey in its original wrap on a tray or in a pan to catch moisture that accumulates as it thaws.

WHOLE TURKEY

8 to 12 pounds	1 to 2 days
12 to 16 pounds	2 to 3 days
16 to 20 pounds	3 to 4 days
20 to 24 pounds	4 to 5 days

PIECES OF LARGE TURKEY

Half, quarter, half breast	1 to 2 days

Thawing a Turkey in Cold Water

If you've left this to the last minute, don't despair. Check the wrapping to make sure there are no tears, and simply place the bird in its unopened bag in the sink or in a large container. Cover with cold water. If the wrapping is torn, place the turkey in another plastic bag, making sure that you close it securely. Change the water frequently to assure safe but effective thawing. The National Turkey Federation recommends every 30 minutes as a rule of thumb.

WHOLE TURKEY

8 to 12 pounds	4 to 6 hours
12 to 16 pounds	6 to 9 hours
16 to 20 pounds	9 to 11 hours
20 to 24 pounds	11 to 12 hours

Source: Adapted from Laura Fox, U.S. Dep't. of Agriculture, Home and Garden Bulletin No. 243.

PUMPKIN CHIFFON PIE

3/4 cup dark brown sugar
1 envelope plain gelatin (1 ounce)
1 teaspoon cinnamon
1/2 teaspoon nutmeg
1/2 teaspoon powdered ginger
1/2 teaspoon salt
1/2 cup milk
1/2 cup water
3 separated eggs
1 cup cooked or canned pumpkin
1/4 cup granulated sugar
Pie crust

Crust: See Pecan–Sweet Potato Pie, page 83, for recipe. Roll out the crust, line a 9- or 10-inch pie plate, and chill for 15 minutes. Line with waxed paper and weigh the crust down with pie weights or beans. Cook in a preheated oven at 375° until browned. Set aside until ready to fill.

Filling: Mix together the brown sugar, gelatin, cinnamon, nutmeg, ginger, and salt. Place in a double boiler over medium heat and add milk, water, beaten egg yolks, and pumpkin. Cook and stir until all ingredients are dissolved and thoroughly heated (the filling should just begin to bubble). Chill until mixture *begins* to set.

Beat the egg whites, gradually adding the sugar, until they are very stiff. Fold gently into the pumpkin mixture, fill the readied pie shell, and chill. Serve with whipped cream or homemade ice cream.

Dishes from Eras Past

*I*t's important to realize that the first Thanksgivings were celebrated with whatever meat—and whatever food—was available. Squash and corn were some of the few vegetables available in winter, salt pork was used constantly, and dried mushrooms, gathered in springtime, might lend an exotic flavor to the scanty ingredients. Butter and milk meant wealth, potatoes were still thought to be poisonous, and most fish was salted in deference to a cold winter sea. Wild game—goose, duck, turkey, smaller birds, squirrel, and venison—highlighted the feasts of early New England.

Because store-bought game is very expensive and much blander than that brought back from the hunt, I've suggested goose, a richly flavored and somewhat neglected bird that makes a meal a feast on any occasion.

ROAST GOOSE WITH APPLE AND PRUNE STUFFING

2 cups prunes
12 pound domestic goose with giblets
2 teaspoons roughly ground black pepper
3 medium shallots
1 tablespoon butter
5 tart apples
1 tablespoon lemon juice
1 onion
1 teaspoon black peppercorns
2 tablespoons flour

Goose and Stuffing: Pit the prunes and allow to plump overnight in 1 cup of boiling water.

Approximately 4 to 5 hours before you plan to serve dinner, remove the neck and giblets from the goose's cavity and set aside in the refrigerator. Trim and reserve excess fat and skin. Rub the cavity with black pepper. Preheat the oven to 375°. Chop the goose's liver and mince the shallots finely. Melt the butter in a sauté pan and cook the shallots briefly, until they just begin to turn translucent. Add the liver and cook for another minute. Remove from heat and place in a mixing bowl with the drained prunes. Peel, core, and quarter the apples, place in the bowl with the prunes, shallots, and liver, and add lemon juice. Stuff the goose's stomach and neck cavity and place it breast side up on a rack in a roasting pan in the oven. Cook the goose for 20 to 30 minutes, until it just begins to brown. Then prick the skin lightly all over and turn the bird over on its breast for 30 minutes at 350°. Lower heat to 300° (lower to 275° if the goose seems to be browning too quickly) and return the goose to a breast-up position, pricking the skin lightly again to release fat. Do this throughout the cooking process and take care to drain and reserve the fat as it accumulates, to prevent it from burning. Cook the goose for 1½ to 2½ more hours in the low oven, until the leg joint is slightly loose when wiggled, the joint juices run clear, and the skin is golden brown. Remove to a platter and let rest for 5 to 10 minutes before removing the stuffing and carving.

Turkey Talk

The turkey is usually praised for the sake of tradition, economy, and the stuffing and sandwiches you can eat the day after the Thanksgiving feast. Most people like it, but few would claim that it packs an absolute wallop of taste. Those who withhold praise for turkey should strive to try a wild turkey one day, a bird that has less in common with its domesticated brother than bologna has with foie gras. Wild turkeys brought from America to France in the seventeenth and eighteenth centuries started a taste craze among the wealthy, who were willing to pay as much as $200 in today's prices for a single *dinde*.

As wild turkeys are still rather dear and difficult to obtain, opt for fresh-killed, free range domesticated birds, with firm, resilient skin that has a hint of pink and real yellow fat to it (see ''Mail-Order Sources,'' page 156). If you've never had one, you'll be stunned by the quality of the taste. Try to avoid turkeys that are saturated in anonymous fats, or punctured by little buttons that erupt when the bird is supposedly done roasting.

Macy's Thanksgiving Book

FRIED OYSTERS

1½ quarts oysters, shucked and drained
2 cups homemade breadcrumbs
1 teaspoon salt
2 teaspoons freshly ground black pepper
4 beaten eggs
1 cup butter or fresh lard

Dry the oysters. Combine breadcrumbs, salt, and pepper. Dip the oysters into the eggs. Lift out and roll through the breadcrumb mixture and place on waxed paper on a tray or plate. Heat the butter or lard over medium to high flame in a skillet before you add the oysters. When the fat is hot brown the oysters on one side and then the other. Serve immediately.

BROILED SHAD ROE

2 pairs shad roe
½ cup olive oil
¼ cup lemon juice
1 minced shallot
Salt
Pepper
¼ teaspoon tabasco sauce
¼ cup butter
Italian parsley, minced

Dry roe carefully (do not remove membrane). Mix together olive oil, lemon juice, shallot, salt, pepper, and tabasco. Soak roe in this marinade for 2 hours, turning from time to time. Melt butter, add parsley, and set aside. Preheat broiler, pour a bit of the marinade on a shallow broiler tray, add the roe and place 3 to 4 inches from the flame. Brown each side, basting with the butter-parsley sauce. Turn only once. Serve on a platter with the remaining butter-parsley sauce.

MORELS IN BUTTER

6 tablespoons butter
1½ cups dried or 4 cups fresh morels
1½ teaspoons Italian parsley, chopped
Freshly ground black pepper
Salt

If using dried morels, place in a bowl, add a pinch of salt, and barely cover with boiling water. Let them sit 3 hours, or until adequately softened. Dry carefully. If using fresh morels, rinse thoroughly in water.

Slice fresh or dried morels to a ⅓-inch width. Sauté with the shallots in the butter over medium heat for about 10 to 12 minutes.

ACORN SQUASH

¼ pound bacon or salt pork, thickly sliced
3 acorn squash, halved and seeded
8 tablespoons butter
Salt to taste
Pepper to taste
½ cup maple syrup

Cook bacon or salt pork until translucent but barely brown. Rub interior of each halved squash with 1 tablespoon of butter and sprinkle with salt and pepper. Place slices of bacon or salt pork in cavity as pictured. Bake on a buttered tray or cookie sheet in a 350° oven for 30 minutes, or until squash begins to soften. Add another tablespoon of butter and 1 to 2 tablespoons of maple syrup to each squash piece. Continue to bake at 400° for 15 minutes and serve immediately. (If bacon is used, it should be served in the squash; salt pork should be discarded.)

JERUSALEM ARTICHOKES

This seldom used but delicious vegetable can be served with either the Simple Vinaigrette or the Mustard Vinaigrette (see pages 70 and 78).

5 cups jerusalem artichokes, sliced
Cold water
1 head Bibb lettuce

Peel the artichokes and chill in cold water to cover for 15 minutes. Slice very thin, toss with the lettuce, and season with vinaigrette.

INDIAN PUDDING

If possible, serve this dish with homemade vanilla ice cream or a good store-bought brand. This pudding tastes exceptionally rich to the modern palate, and the contrast in temperature and flavor is sensational.

1 cup yellow corn meal
¼ cup sugar
½ cup dark molasses
2 eggs
¼ teaspoon powdered ginger
¼ teaspoon baking soda
¼ teaspoon salt
1½ quarts hot milk
¼ cup butter

Mix the ingredients thoroughly with half of the hot milk. Place in a buttered bean pot (or any high-sided, solid stoneware baking dish) and bake in a hot (425° to 450°) oven until the mixture boils. Stir in the remaining milk and bake at 275° to 300° for another 4 to 6 hours, uncovered. Serve hot.

A Holiday Buffet

*T*his buffet could easily serve as a sit-down meal. The recipes do not have to be served hot, and they do not require carving at the table or a good deal of cutting on the plate. You should avoid such things, along with food that is difficult to maneuver (large chunks of leaf lettuce), might roll (brussels sprouts), stain (braised beets or a red wine stew), or wash over the side of the plate (oyster stew) for any buffet menu, whether people will be sitting or standing while they eat.

DUCK BREASTS WITH APPLES COOKED IN CIDER AND APPLEJACK

4 separate moulard or muscovy duck breasts (8 breasts if Long Island ducklings are used)

Marinade:
1 cup dijon mustard
2 cups white wine
1 teaspoon allspice
1/2 teaspoon clove
1/2 teaspoon roughly ground black peppercorns
4 bay leaves

Stewed Apples:
8 tart green or pie apples
1 quart unpasteurized cider
3/4 cup applejack
1/2 cup cider vinegar
3 tablespoons brown sugar
1/3 cup currants

Duck Breasts: Dry duck breasts carefully and place in a lidded crock or bowl. If whole carcasses are used, reserve backbone, wings, and giblets for soup or sauce stock; legs and thighs for hash, soup, confit, or a myriad of other uses. Mix together the marinade ingredients, pour over the duck, and refrigerate, covered, for two days.

Approximately 30 to 45 minutes before serving, remove breasts from the marinade (which can be discarded). Wipe off most of the paste, leaving a thin film of marinade. Score the fat side of the breasts and heat a heavy skillet over a medium flame. Use no oil or fat. When the pan is hot, fry the duck breast-side down for 5 minutes, or until the skin is a deep golden brown. Turn and sear the other side over high heat for 1 to 2 minutes. Place the skillet in a preheated 400° oven, skin-side up, and roast for an additional 10 minutes. (The cooking times can be halved with Long Island ducklings.) Remove from the oven and slice immediately to prevent the breasts from stiffening and continuing to cook. Cut on the bias, 1/2-inch to 1/3-inch thick slices, and arrange on a platter rimmed with the stewed apples. The breasts do not have to be served hot, but they should be served within a half hour.

Stewed Apples: Peel, core, and quarter apples. Mix together cider, 1/2 cup of the applejack, and cider vinegar in a deep saucepan. Bring liquid to a boil, add apples, return to a simmer, and cook 8 to 10 minutes, turning apples if liquid does not cover them. Drain apples, discarding all but 3/4 cup of the liquid. Add brown sugar, an additional 1/4 cup applejack, and currants and cook over high heat for about 2 minutes until the liquid begins to glaze. Remove from heat. Arrange the quartered apples and duck-breast slices on the platter and drizzle the glaze over the apples.

RED CABBAGE WITH PANCETTA

1 6-inch to 8-inch head of red cabbage
1/2 pound pancetta or hickory-smoked bacon
1/4 to 1/3 cup red-wine vinegar
1 1/2 teaspoons sugar

Slice the cabbage thinly (do not grate). Slice the pancetta or bacon into 1-inch long, 1/3-inch thick slices and cook over low heat in a large sauté pan. When the meat is done, pour off some of the fat and add the cabbage to the sauté pan, cooking over medium heat until the cabbage is tender but not limp. Sprinkle the vinegar and sugar over the top, stir thoroughly, and cook for 2 to 3 minutes, or until some of the vinegar has cooked off. Serve immediately.

SCALLOPED POTATOES

6 small or 4 medium leeks
3 pounds red new potatoes
1/4 cup butter (or duck or goose fat)
1/2 teaspoon thyme
Salt to taste
Freshly ground black pepper to taste
1 cup thinly sliced strips of firm ham or prosciutto
1 cup chicken stock
2/3 cup heavy cream

Grease the bottom of a shallow 3-quart baking dish. Clean leeks carefully and chop. Slice potatoes into 1/4-inch thins. Quickly sauté the leeks in the butter adding the thyme and seasoning liberally with salt and pepper. Layer the baking dish first with the potatoes, then with the leek mixture, and then the ham. Repeat the layering process and top with potatoes. Pour the heated chicken stock over the potatoes and bake in a 325° oven for 30 minutes. Pour on the cream and bake for another hour.

LOBSTER CAESAR SALAD

2 lobsters
3 garlic cloves
3/4 cup light olive oil
2 cups cubed semolina or french bread
1 large head romaine lettuce
1/3 cup extra-virgin olive oil
1 tin anchovies (about 10 to 12 fillets)
2 tablespoons fresh-squeezed lemon juice
1 teaspoon kosher salt, or to taste
1 teaspoon freshly ground black pepper
1 egg
3/4 cup freshly grated parmesan (reggiano)

Bring a large pot of salted water to a rapid boil and quickly immerse live lobsters, head first. Cover, return to a boil, and cook for 7 to 8 minutes if they are 2-pound lobsters, 2 minutes less or more for each half pound. Remove lobsters and place on their backs; split end to end with heavy shears or a large knife (don't hesitate to use a mallet with the knife if necessary). Save the tomalley (the green liver) and the coral roe (if there is any) and set aside.

Halve the garlic cloves and place in a heavy skillet with the light olive oil. Place over a medium flame and add the cubed bread when the oil is hot. Turn the croutons as they become golden brown, so that all sides are evenly colored. It is important to be attentive, as they will burn easily. When done, drain on paper towels and set aside.

Wash and trim romaine and dry thoroughly. Rip into largish pieces and place in a large salad bowl. Tear or slice the lobster tail and claw meat into 1 to 1 1/2 inch pieces and add to the romaine. Pour on the extra-virgin olive oil and toss thoroughly so that the romaine and lobster are evenly coated. Add the anchovies, lemon juice, salt, and pepper. Toss well again. Drop in the croutons and drizzle the well-whisked egg (and 1 tablespoon each of tomalley and roe, if desired) and toss again. Finally, add the parmesan, toss again, correct seasoning and serve.

SHRIMP WITH CURRY MAYONNAISE

Shrimp:
2 bay leaves
1 teaspoon thyme
3 pounds shrimp
1 teaspoon black peppercorns

Curry Mayonnaise:
2 cups mayonnaise
1 1/2 tablespoons hot curry powder

Bring two gallons of lightly salted water to a rolling boil with bay leaves, thyme, and peppercorns. Add the unshelled shrimp and allow the water to return to a rolling boil. Remove from heat and let the shrimp remain in the water for five minutes before removing and rinsing with cold water. Chill before shelling and arranging on a platter. Add the curry powder to the prepared mayonnaise and stir carefully. Let sit, refrigerated, before adjusting seasoning and serving.

MAYONNAISE

Mayonnaise will usually thicken slightly in the hour or so after it is finished. This recipe yields about 2 cups.

3 egg yolks
1 teaspoon salt
1/2 teaspoon ground white pepper
1/2 teaspoon dry mustard
2 tablespoons lemon juice or 1 tablespoon vinegar
1 3/4 cups olive oil

Whisk egg yolks, salt, pepper, mustard, and lemon juice vigorously in a bowl until well blended. (A rotary beater, food processor, or blender are easier but less exact options.) Add the oil drop by drop, whisking hard until the mayonnaise begins to emulsify and thicken. As it begins to do so the remaining oil can be added more rapidly, but take care that it emulsifies before each addition. If the mayonnaise is too thick when completed, thin gradually with lemon juice. If it breaks, start with new egg yolks in another bowl, add a bit of oil drop by drop, and then add the curdled mayonnaise very gradually.

POACHED VEGETABLES IN VINAIGRETTE

For this recipe you can use any combination of fresh green beans, new potatoes, peas, baby carrots, celeriac, asparagus, snow peas, artichoke hearts, beets, broccoli, and cauliflower. Fresh mushrooms, scallions, and cherry tomatoes are good additions; add tuna, egg, leaf lettuce, and anchovies and you have salad niçoise. All vegetables should be firm to the bite after simmering or steaming but not so *al dente* as to be stringy.

This vinaigrette will keep in the refrigerator for about a week.

Mustard Vinaigrette:
1/4 cup champagne vinegar
1/4 cup dijon mustard
2 egg yolks
1 teaspoon freshly ground black pepper
1/2 teaspoon salt
1/4 teaspoon sugar
1 clove pressed garlic
1/4 teaspoon thyme (1/2 teaspoon fresh, if possible)
1 cup extra-virgin olive oil

Whisk vinegar, mustard, yolks, and all the other ingredients except the oil until very smooth. Add the olive oil gradually, whisking constantly. This is not a mayonnaise, but it should be thick and creamy, able to stand for at least an hour without separating. If it does separate, it can be brought back by whisking or shaking. Adjust seasonings and dress poached and fresh vegetables. Serve in a bowl lined plentifully with red leaf lettuce.

A Holiday Buffet

LEMON MERINGUE PIE

Zest and juice of two large lemons
1 1/2 cups sugar
2 heaping tablespoons flour
3 eggs, separated
1 1/2 cups water
1 scant tablespoon butter
Pie shell (see page 83)
6 tablespoons sugar (for meringue)

Grate the lemon zest and add to the blended sugar and flour. Add egg yolks, lemon juice, water, and butter and beat well. Cook over low to medium heat in a heavy saucepan until the mixture thickens to the consistency of cold honey. Chill before filling prebaked pie shell.

Beat egg whites until stiff, then gradually add sugar. Spoon chilled lemon mixture into the prebaked pie shell, dollop and spread the meringue on top, and bake for 15 minutes at 325°.

CHEESE AND FRUIT

Buy about 1/2 pound of three different cheeses. Try to select a variety: a good sharp cheddar or Cheshire or nutty aged gouda; a creamy French blue or a wedge of Stilton; a redolent Camembert or fresh and mild goat cheese. Always allow the cheese to reach room temperature before serving and never preslice it—simply place a knife next to each and surround with good, fresh bread, crackers, and grapes, plums, clementines, or any variety of small fruit.

> A good cheddar needn't be from Vermont, but real Vermont cheddar sums up the best qualities of the old English cheese: it is well-aged, sharp, crumbly, and never sour. Wisconsin-style cheddar shares these qualities, though it is dyed orange, and in a pinch some commercial brands, notably Cracker Barrel Extra Sharp, will do fine.

Regional Specialties

This is a regional menu true to no particular region, but blending characteristics of several areas that complement one another. Roast capon with a cornbread stuffing stems from the Maryland/Virginia area; black-eyed peas and pecan-and-sweet potato pie from the deep south states of Georgia and Louisiana; compote recipes were first published in Philadelphia, although they're made throughout the union; oyster stew is a New England mainstay; and brussels sprouts with vinegar are popular in the German and Scandinavian families of the Midwest, even though the recipe is also an old English one. And for a southwest flavor try the Cornbread and Jalapeño dressing from Texarkana (page 95).

ROAST CAPON

6-pound capon
8 tablespoons butter
1 teaspoon rosemary

Preheat oven to 375°. Stuff capon and place on a rack in a shallow roasting pan. Start it on its side and turn it to its other side after 30 minutes. Baste with melted butter seasoned with the rosemary. Place it on its back after another 30 minutes, baste again, and continue basting with butter and pan juices at 20-minute intervals. Allow 20 to 25 minutes a pound for cooking time, but check the thigh joint after 2 hours. Remove when the juices are clear but still tinged with pink. Let rest 10 minutes before removing the stuffing and carving.

CORN BREAD, CHESTNUT, AND SAUSAGE STUFFING

1 cup chestnuts
1 large onion, finely chopped
10 tablespoons butter
1/2 pound lean pork sausage
Finely chopped capon's liver
6 cups corn bread, crumbled roughly
1/3 cup white wine
2 tablespoons chive
1 teaspoon thyme
1/2 teaspoon rosemary
1 teaspoon pepper
1 teaspoon salt

Wash and drain the chestnuts if they're canned. If they're fresh, simmer them for 20 minutes, allow them to cool, then peel them. For uniform pieces, use a knife and chop the nut meats; for a different effect, though, you can break the chestnuts. Put the chestnuts in a bag and whack them with a rolling pin.

Sauté onion in 2 tablespoons of butter in a large skillet until translucent. Remove onion to a bowl and add sausage to the skillet, breaking it up as you brown it. Brown over medium heat for 5 minutes before adding liver and chestnuts. Cook for another 2 minutes, remove from heat, and blend with onion and other ingredients in a mixing bowl. Adjust seasonings.

Macy's Thanksgiving Book

DEVILED OYSTER STEW

5 tablespoons butter
3/4 cup milk
1/2 cup cream
2 tablespoons chopped shallots
3/4 cup oyster liquid or broth
1/4 teaspoon dry mustard
1/4 teaspoon nutmeg
Salt
Pepper
2 pints oysters
1 cup dried, buttered breadcrumbs
1/2 teaspoon red-pepper flakes
2 tablespoons chopped parsley

Melt 3 tablespoons butter and add milk, cream, shallots, and oyster liquid. Mix, then add mustard, nutmeg, salt, and pepper to taste. Bring liquid to a boil, reduce heat, add oysters, and let simmer 2 minutes. Pour into a buttered baking dish. Melt remaining butter and add 1/4-inch layer of breadcrumbs, red pepper, and parsley. Stir until crumbs are moistened, spread on top of the stew mixture and bake at 375° for 15 minutes, or until crumbs are golden. Serve immediately.

BRUSSELS SPROUTS AND MALT VINEGAR

4 cups brussels sprouts
2 tablespoons butter
1/2 cup broken walnut meats
3/4 cup malt vinegar

Trim the brussels sprouts of outer leaves and stem ends. Bring a small pot of lightly salted water to a boil, add the sprouts, and cook for 2 to 3 minutes, depending on size. Drain and sauté in butter over fairly high heat for another 3 minutes or until they are tender but still firm when a fork prong is inserted. Place in a serving dish and sprinkle with 1/4 cup of the vinegar, reserving the rest for a cruet at the table. Serve immediately.

PECAN-SWEET POTATO PIE

Dough:
3 1/8 cups flour
1 cup lard or shortening
1 teaspoon salt
1/2 cup very cold water

Sweet Potato Filling:
1 cup cooked sweet potato pulp (2 or 3 medium yams)
1/2 cup dark brown sugar
1 tablespoon heavy cream
1 tablespoon bourbon
1 tablespoon softened butter
1 tablespoon vanilla extract
1/2 teaspoon cinnamon
1/4 teaspoon freshly grated nutmeg
1/2 teaspoon salt

Pecan Filling:
3/4 cup dark brown sugar
3/4 cup dark corn syrup
1 1/2 tablespoons butter, melted
2 eggs, beaten
1/2 teaspoon salt
2 teaspoons vanilla
1 cup pecan halves

Crust: Blend flour, lard, and salt well; then add cold water. Blend with fingers—handling the dough as little as possible—until it is crumbly, until it just holds its shape. A few more drops of water may be necessary. When the water is incorporated, let dough rest in a patty and refrigerate. After it rests for 15 minutes, divide it into two pieces and roll out 1/8-inch thin onto a generously floured surface. Fit into a pie plate, allowing some overlap on the edges for baking shrinkage, and chill in the refrigerator.

Filling: Bake sweet potatoes in a 350° oven for 30 to 45 minutes or until tender. Let cool slightly, then combine sieved pulp and other sweet potato filling ingredients, beating well until smooth. Set aside. Combine the pecan filling ingredients—except the nuts—beating until the syrup is smooth and glossy.

Spoon and smooth the sweet potato filling over the bottom of the crust. Arrange pecan halves on top and pour pecan syrup carefully up to the rim of the crust. Bake at 325° for 1 1/2 hours or until a knife inserted in the center comes out cleanly.

BLACK-EYED PEAS WITH HAM AND RED PEPPERS

2 cups black-eyed peas, soaked overnight in water
1/4 cup ham fat
1 cup white rice
1 cup roughly chopped ham
1 bunch scallions, chopped
2 red bell peppers, chopped
1 teaspoon coarsely ground black pepper
2 tablespoons butter
Pinch of salt

After soaking in a colander, drain and rinse peas. Place in a pot with the ham fat, cover with cold water, and simmer until the beans are tender, from 2 to 3 hours. Discard any undissolved fat but reserve 2 1/2 cups cooking liquid. Add water if necessary. Bring cooking liquid to a boil in a separate saucepan. Add half the peas and all the rice, cover, and simmer over low heat until the rice is tender, approximately 20 to 25 minutes.

Sauté ham, scallions, red peppers, and pepper in a skillet with butter. When the red peppers are tender, combine with remaining peas and rice-and-peas mixture; salt to taste and serve.

The Children's Corner

C hildren will eat anything and nothing at the same time. Cravings define appetite, and no parent can prescribe what will be craved. Some children love stuffing and turkey and shrimp and spoonbread and salad, some hate all of the above but yearn for duck a l'orange. Most loathe mixing things together on their plate, and in this rather arbitrary section I've listed some options that are fairly self-contained and simple in flavor.

TWICE-BAKED POTATOES

6 medium baking potatoes
1 cup sour cream
1/3 cup Vermont cheddar or 1/4 cup parmesan
1/2 teaspoon salt
1/2 teaspoon pepper
1/2 teaspoon paprika

Scrub potatoes, dry, and puncture with a fork to let steam escape while baking. Bake at 375° until tender, 30 to 45 minutes depending on size. Remove from oven and let cool. Cut the top off each potato, leaving a lengthwise boat shape. Scrape the potato pulp out, leaving the boat of skin intact. In a mixing bowl blend the potato with sour cream, cheese, and seasonings. Mix well, but leave some lumps. Fill the shells and bake on a lightly greased baking sheet, with the oven still on 375°, for 15 minutes or until the tops are golden.

GLAZED HAM

5-pound smoked and cured ham, butt end
2/3 cup brown sugar
3/4 cup crushed fresh pineapple
1 teaspoon powdered cloves
1/2 teaspoon dry mustard

Place ham in an iron skillet and begin baking in a 350° oven. Score fat on the top in a diamond or star pattern, as shown, so that the ham will brown more easily. For the glaze, bring the other ingredients to a simmer in a saucepan and remove from heat.

When the ham has baked for 1 to 1 1/4 hours, remove from oven and coat with the glaze. Raise the temperature to 375° and bake for another 30 minutes.

Remove ham from the skillet to a platter and let rest 5 to 10 minutes. Pour off the fat in the pan but reserve the drippings. Deglaze with a little water or vinegar and thicken with flour or water (see page 67).

APPLESAUCE

10 tart apples
1 cup cider
1 cup water
3/4 cup brown sugar
2 teaspoons cinnamon
1/2 teaspoon vanilla
1/2 teaspoon salt
1/4 cup red hot candies (red cinnamon hearts)

Peel, core, and dice the apples. Place in a heavy enamel saucepan with the cider, water, and sugar and begin to cook over a medium flame, lowering the heat and mashing the apples as they grow soft. When the mixture is smooth (about 10 minutes), add the cinnamon, vanilla, and salt and chill in the refrigerator. Add the red hots a few minutes before serving and swirl the applesauce in the bowl so that the dissolving candies streak the mixture.

STEAMED ARTICHOKES

Do not use an aluminum pot for this recipe, as the artichokes may discolor.

6 medium artichokes
2 tablespoons fresh-squeezed lemon juice
1 tablespoon olive oil
8 tablespoons butter, melted

Trim artichoke stem to 1/2 inch and remove the top layer of outer leaves. Place in a covered pot with 2 inches of water, 1 tablespoon lemon juice, and the olive oil. Simmer for 30 to 45 minutes, until the stem is tender but firm when checked with a fork prong. Drain and dry. Use the remaining lemon juice and butter for a dipping sauce.

Variation: Chill and serve with a lemon mayonnaise— 1 tablespoon lemon juice mixed with one cup homemade (see page 77) or 3/4 cup store-bought mayonnaise.

GINGERBREAD

1/4 cup dark brown sugar
1 egg
3/4 cup dark molasses
1/2 cup butter
1/4 cup milk
1/2 cup sour cream
2 1/2 cups flour
1 teaspoon baking powder
1/2 teaspoon baking soda
1 teaspoon ginger
3/4 teaspoon cinnamon
1/2 teaspoon cloves
1/2 teaspoon salt

Beat together the sugar, egg, molasses and softened butter. Gradually add milk and sour cream and blend well. Sift together the flour and other dry ingredients; add slowly to the wet ingredients, blending well to prevent lumping. Pour into a buttered and floured 8-inch by 8-inch baking pan and bake in a preheated 350° oven for 30 minutes (or until cake tests done in the center and begins to shrink from the sides of the pan). Serve warm with fresh whipped cream.

Variation: If the gingerbread is being served to adults, try adding 2 tablespoons of grated semisweet chocolate and 1 tablespoon dark rum to the cream once it is whipped.

The Children's Corner

Luscious Leftovers

Sandwiches are the obvious winner in this category—grilled or cold, packed with stuffing or simply breast meat and mayonnaise, layered with lettuce or cheese or thinly sliced onion, and dolloped with everything from cranberry to horseradish. This section is meant to help transform less obvious leftovers—the overload of the refrigerator (extra unprepared potatoes and onions, fruit, cheese, and cream) and the table (leftover bread, stock, rice, cooked shrimp, stuffing, and dark meat)—into recipes that can stand as a feast in their own right.

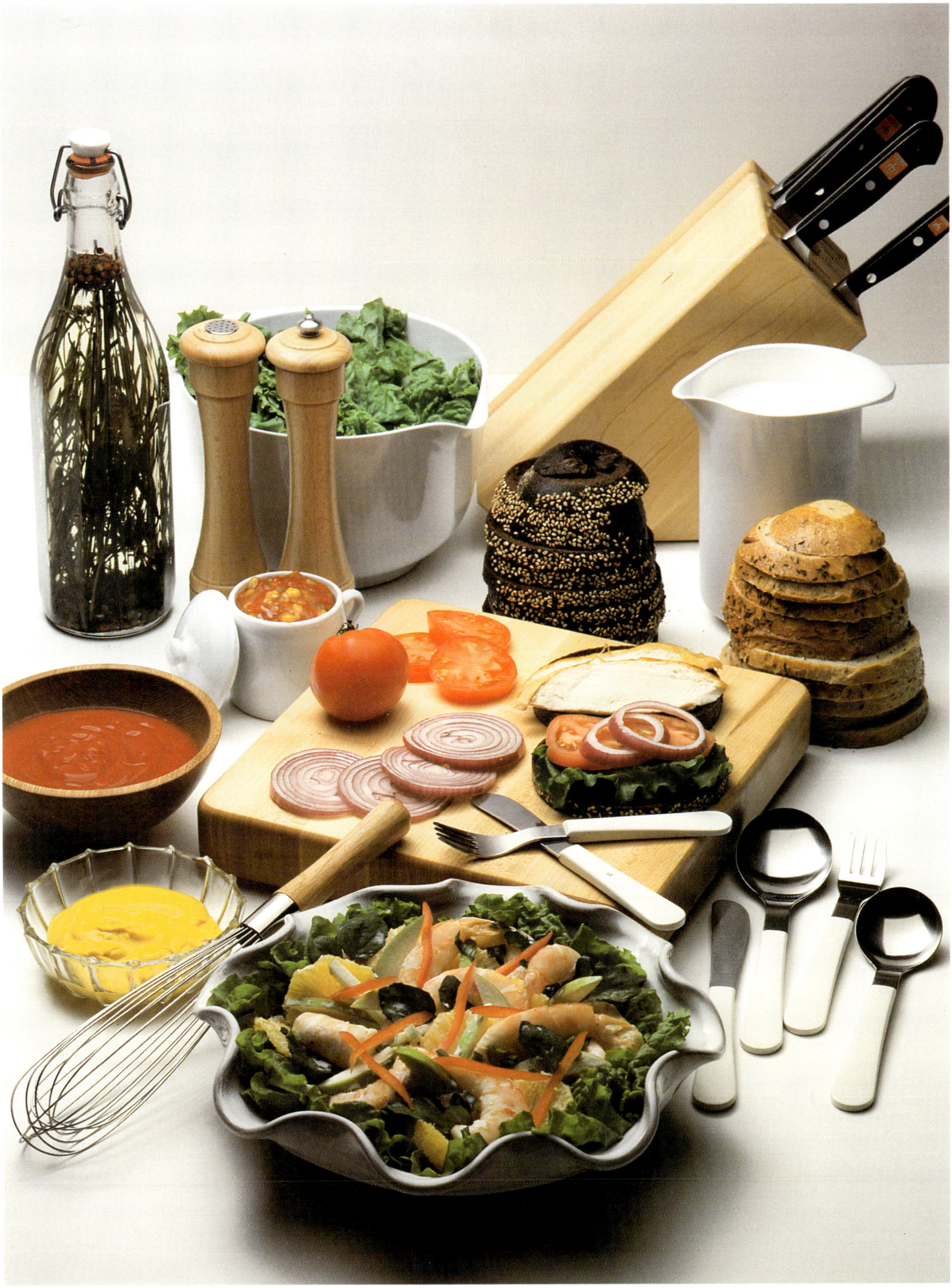

BIRD HASH

(Use turkey, goose, duck, capon, or leftover ham.)

2/3 cup duck or goose cracklings
2 medium onions, thinly sliced
2 cups thinly sliced russet potatoes
3 cups cooked poultry, diced large
1 teaspoon tabasco
1 1/2 teaspoon freshly ground pepper
1 teaspoon salt
1/2 cup leftover goose stuffing (apples and prunes
2 tablespoons chopped parsley
Duck or goose fat for sautéing (or 2 tablespoons butter)

Crisp duck or goose cracklings (fat and skin cut into thin strips) in some of their own fat in a small skillet. Drain the cracklings on paper towel and set aside. Transfer the fat or butter to a large skillet, adding more if necessary to cover the bottom of the skillet. Add the onions and potatoes when the fat is hot. When the onions are tender and begin to brown, add the poultry, tabasco, pepper, salt, and stuffing. Cook for another 5 minutes and serve garnished with parsley and cracklings.

SHRIMP, ORANGE, AND APPLE SALAD

3 large scallions
10 sprigs watercress
2 large green apples
3 seville oranges
1 1/2 pounds medium shrimp
1/3 cup cognac
1/4 cup sherry
1/2 teaspoon tabasco sauce
Kosher salt
Freshly ground black pepper
2 1/2 cups mayonnaise
Red-leaf lettuce
1 red pepper, julienned

Chop scallions and break watercress into 2-inch sprigs. Peel, core, and julienne the apples; finely grate the zest of one orange, squeeze its juice and set the juice aside. Peel the remaining two oranges and slice thinly. Mix together scallions, watercress, apples, and orange slices and zest and refrigerate. Bring a large pot of water to a boil, add shrimp, and remove after the water has returned to a boil for one minute. Rinse in cold water, shell, and devein if necessary. Mix together the cognac, sherry, orange juice, tabasco, salt and pepper and pour over the shrimp. Let marinate for two hours, then mix with the fruit, watercress, and scallions and fold in the mayonnaise. Line a bowl with red-leaf lettuce, spoon in the shrimp, and decorate with the julienned red pepper. Serve immediately.

SOUP STOCK

Poultry carcass
Giblets and neck (if not already used in gravy stock)
2 onions, halved
2 carrots, halved
1 bunch parsley
1 tablespoon black peppercorns
3 bay leaves
1 teaspoon tarragon
1 teaspoon thyme
1 small, unpeeled head of garlinc
any leftover leek greens or uncooked rutabaga
1/4 cup white wine
Salt
Pepper

Place all ingredients but the wine, salt, and pepper in a large stockpot and add cold water to cover. Simmer on low heat for two hours, adding water only if absolutely necessary, and then only in the first hour. Strain stock and discard solids.

Add the wine and season the liquid with salt and pepper. Reduce and season until you have a good broth.

Add chunked goose, duck, turkey or chicken leg meat, or goose or duck breast meat to the finished stock. Add any leftover cooked wild rice (or thinly sliced new potatoes if there are no leftovers), thinly sliced sauteed red onion, and a sprig of thyme. Simmer for 10 minutes and serve.

BREAD PUDDING

Bread Pudding:
3 eggs
1 1/2 cups light brown sugar
1 quart milk
6 tablespoons butter, melted
5 tablespoons vanilla
1 loaf french or semolina bread, cubed and dried (5 or 6 cups)
1 scant teaspoon freshly grated or 1/2 teaspoon powdered nutmeg

Bourbon Sauce:
8 tablspoons butter
1 cup light brown sugar
1 large egg, well beaten
Pinch of salt
5 tablespoons bourbon
1 teaspoon vanilla

Bread Pudding: Whisk eggs and sugar thoroughly. Blend in milk, butter, and vanilla, toss in raisins, and let plump for 15 minutes. Add the bread and nutmeg and soak until the bread is thoroughly moistened. (The staler the bread, the better, as it will keep its shape and texture as the pudding cooks; 1-inch cubes are best.)

Pat the pudding into a buttered baking pan, and place in an oven preheated to 350°. Immediately reduce the heat to 300° and let bake for 30 minutes. Remove from oven, stir thoroughly, replace in oven, and raise temperature back to 350°. Bake for another 20 to 30 minutes, or until nicely browned. Let the pudding cool before you cut it. Place it on dessert plates and top with warm bourbon sauce.

Bourbon Sauce: Beat the butter and sugar until very creamy and heat it in a double boiler or heavy enamel saucepan until dissolved and quite hot. Add the egg and salt, whipping fast to prevent curdling. Let cool slightly before whipping in the bourbon and vanilla.

SPOONBREAD WITH HAM AND GRUYERE

1 cup fine white cornmeal
1 1/2 teaspoons sugar
1 teaspoon baking powder
1/2 teaspoon baking soda
1/2 teaspoon salt
2 medium eggs, beaten
2 cups buttermilk
1/2 cup thinly sliced ham
1/2 cup grated gruyere or Vermont cheddar
3 tablespoons butter

Sift dry ingredients and add eggs, beating vigorously. Add buttermilk, beating well again, and incorporate the ham and cheese. Pour into a well-buttered baking dish and bake for 35 to 40 minutes in a preheated 400° oven. Remove from oven, top with pats of butter, and serve immediately.

Gifts to Bring

*T*he variety of gifts you can give in the fall largely depends on how much ''putting up'' you do in the summer when the ingredients are plentiful and inexpensive. The recipes included in this section are not reliant on short-seasoned fruits and vegetables, such as berries and peaches, asparagus and green tomatoes. The vinegars and preserved fruits in alcohol are not dependent on a season, although some of the most delicious variations are best prepared in summertime. The choices here are for everyone to make when they have a moment prior to the hectic activity of the feast itself.

The pound cake will last about two weeks and is prime with the soft flavor of bourbon at about one week. Mincemeat will keep for months and can be used as a relish as well as for Thanksgiving and Christmas pies. The compote, stored in the refrigerator, will be tasty for a month, and the fruits in brandy will keep indefinitely, as will the vinegars if they are stored away from the sun.

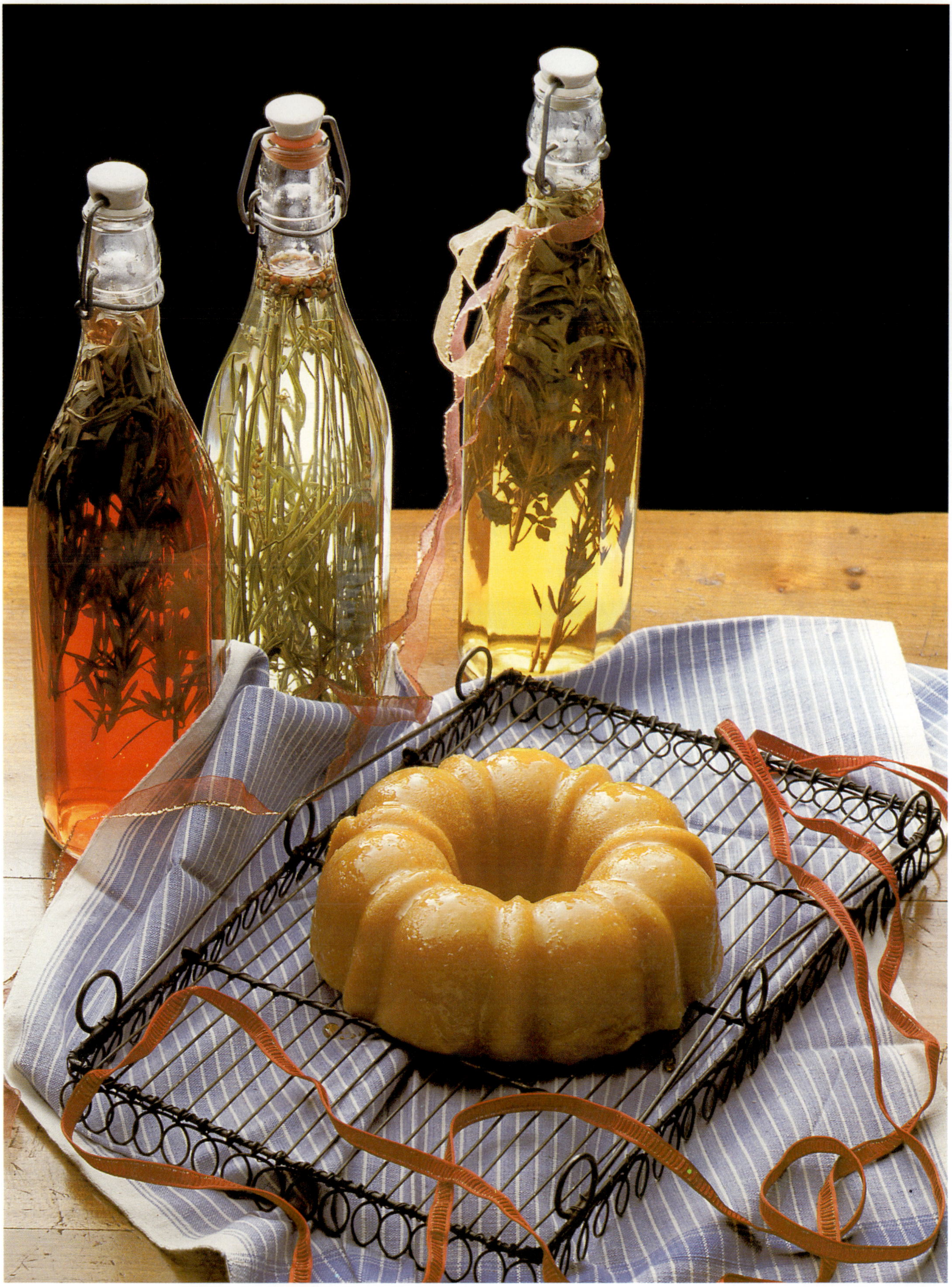

DRUNKEN POUND CAKE

Cake:
3 1/2 cups all-purpose flour, sifted
2 teaspoons baking powder
1 1/2 cups butter, softened
2 1/2 cups light brown sugar
1/2 cup dark brown sugar
1 tablespoon vanilla
1/2 teaspoon ginger
1/2 teaspoon cloves
1/2 teaspoon salt
5 large eggs
1/2 cup bourbon
1/2 cup milk or half and half
Cornmeal or breadcrumbs

Glaze:
1/3 cup granulated sugar
1/3 cup bourbon
Juice of one lemon

Cake: Sift flour and baking powder together and set aside. Butter a 10-inch by 4-inch tube pan and line the bottom with wax paper. Butter the paper and dust the pan with fine cornmeal or breadcrumbs.

In a clean bowl, cream butter and sugar until light and fluffy. Add vanilla, ginger, cloves, and salt; then add the eggs, one at a time, beating well after each addition. Add sifted dry ingredients gradually, alternating with blended bourbon and milk. When all ingredients are well incorporated, pour the batter into the prepared tube pan, tapping the pan gently to make sure that the batter is level.

Bake at 350° for 1 hour and 20 minutes or until the cake is springy to the touch and a toothpick comes out dry. Cool for 15 minutes before inverting, putting on a plate, and glazing. Let the pound cake sit overnight before slicing. It will last for a week or so if tightly sealed to prevent drying.

Glaze: Dissolve sugar, bourbon, and lemon juice in a small saucepan over low heat. Baste the cake with the glaze while both are still warm.

PEAR-AND-CRANBERRY COMPOTE

4 large pears
1 cup water
1/2 cup cider
1/4 cup bourbon
1 cup dark brown sugar
Zest and juice of 1 lemon
1 1/2 cups cranberries

Peel, core, and cut each pear into 6 pieces. Mix together water, cider, bourbon, sugar, and lemon zest and juice. Bring to a simmer, add cranberries, simmer for 2 minutes, and add pears. Cook—no more than 4 minutes—until tender but not mushy and place in a serving bowl. Cook the syrup for another 2 minutes, pour over fruit, and serve.

CRANBERRY BREAD

1 cup roughly chopped raw cranberries
2 cups flour
1 cup sugar
1/2 teaspoon salt
1/2 teaspoon baking soda
1/2 teaspoon baking powder
2 tablespoons shortening
1 egg
Juice and rind of 1 orange
Boiling water

Freeze the cranberries in their bag before you chop them—they'll lose less juice.

Sift together the flour, sugar, salt, baking soda, and baking powder and set aside. In a measuring cup, place the shortening and the juice and grated rind of the orange (be careful not to include the white pulp). Add boiling water to the 3/4-cup mark. Add to the sifted dry ingredients with the egg and cranberries. Blend well and pour into a greased 8-inch by 4-inch loaf pan. Bake at 350° for 1 hour.

FRUITS IN BRANDY

This gift is simple to prepare, but time must be allowed for the fruit to be flavored by the alcohol and flavor it in turn, and the alcohol itself is expensive. The drawbacks are worth it—brandied fruit can be used for a huge variety of desserts and savories. Soak peaches in cognac and serve the result with grated semisweet chocolate and whipped cream flavored with the liquor. Serve pears in poire next to a roast pork loin or use them in the glaze; layer apples in calvados or applejack on the bottom of a custard tart; serve raspberries in framboise over chocolate mousse. Your options are only limited by your imagination and your wallet and the fruits available.

2 quarts fresh fruit, unblemished—try blackberries, raspberries, or black or red cherries (strawberries tend to lose color and become rubbery); apples; pears; plums; or peaches (peeled but not cored or pitted)
1 fifth appropriate brandy, cognac, or armagnac

Make sure that the fruit is clean and ripe but still quite firm. Place into a sterilized glass or pottery container, add the alcohol, and seal carefully. Allow to rest refrigerated or in a cool, dark room for one month before using.

TEXAS TOFFEE

10 tablespoons butter
1 cup brown sugar
1 cup walnuts or pecans, finely chopped
8 ounces semisweet chocolate, grated

Combine and cook the butter and sugar over medium heat, stirring constantly, until a candy thermometer registers 288°. Pour over the finely chopped nuts in a buttered 9-inch by 9-inch pan. Sprinkle the top with the grated chocolate immediately—it can be spread as it melts. Let cool on a rack and break into pieces, or score the candy into squares when half-hardened.

VINEGARS

There are two ways of making vinegars: You can make your own by fermenting a "mother" solution; or you can flavor plain vinegar, changing it entirely. The first requires special equipment, patience, and time, but the second is ridiculously easy. The best herbs to use are tarragon, thyme, oregano and marjoram. Nasturtiums are beautiful and lend the vinegar a delicious sharp, peppery flavor. Wild leeks or ramps are best of all, but shallots are easier to find and have some of the same flavor.

1 gallon white distilled vinegar
1 1/2 cups fresh herbs on the branch

Heat the vinegar to a simmer in a large pot (not aluminum, which may cause an unwanted chemical reaction). Add the herbs and remove from heat. Let the mixture cool and place in a large, covered jar. Let it steep for 2 weeks before straining through cheesecloth and placing in individual lidded bottles. Insert fresh herb sprigs for show.

MINCEMEAT

2 pounds lean beef (bottom round)
1/2 pound veal kidney suet
1/2 pound currants
1/4 pound golden raisins
1/4 pound dark raisins
3 cups green apples, diced small
Juice of 1 orange and grated rind of 2
Juice of 1 lemon and grated rind of 2
1 teaspoon each cinnamon, allspice, cloves, nutmeg, salt
1 cup dark brown sugar
1 cup each rum, brandy, madeira

Cook the beef thoroughly, either by simmering or roasting. Chop beef and suet fine and put through a meat grinder. Mix all nonalcoholic ingredients together until blended. Add the alcohol. Keep in covered stone or glass containers and store in a dark, cold, dry place. Allow 3 weeks to age before using.

De Gustibus — Macy's Cooking School

Arlene Feltman, director of De Gustibus at Macy's, with five illustrious French chefs.

Many of the world's great chefs have presented their recipes and preparation methods in the De Gustibus at Macy's cooking school. Some of these renowned cooks have graciously offered their favorite dishes to enhance your holiday dinner.

ALAIN SAILHAC'S EGGPLANT AND SPINACH CAKE

Eggplant and Spinach Cake:
8 ounces fresh spinach
4 tablespoons butter
1 tablespoon water
10 ounces eggplant
6 ounces red pepper
Salt to taste
Pepper to taste
Herbes de Provence to taste

Tomato Coulis:
1 (6 ounce) tomato, peeled
¹/₂ teaspoon chopped shallots
¹/₂ teaspoon olive oil
Salt to taste
Pepper to taste

Eggplant and Spinach Cake: Cook spinach for 2 minutes with one teaspoon of butter and one tablespoon of water. Add salt and pepper to taste. Drain spinach and set aside. Slice the eggplant; do not peel. Fry for 3 minutes. Add salt and pepper to taste. Dry on napkins or paper towels. Set aside. Peel the red pepper and dice. Cook slowly over low heat until all the moisture disappears. Add salt and pepper according to taste, plus a little herbes de Provence.

Tomato Coulis: Dice tomato and discard seeds. Heat shallots in a pan with butter for 2 minutes. Add diced tomatoes, salt, pepper, and cook for 5 minutes. Blend in a blender or small food processor for 15 seconds.

Place the cake in the serving dish. Pour the coulis into the dish so it surrounds the cake. Serves 2.

RICHARD LAVIN'S STUFFED SNOW PEAS

36 snow peas
¹/₂ pound cheese, softened chèvre or boursin
1 tomato

Clean snow peas and slice off one end of pea with knife. Blanch in vigorously boiling water about 30 seconds; cool in an ice bath. Drain water and dry peas on towel. With pastry bag, pipe softened cheese into peas. Pipe a large circle of cheese on serving platter. Arrange snow peas on platter like the spokes of a wheel, side-by-side and touching each other. Use the cheese circle to hold them in place. (Figure on 3 or 4 pea pods per person. Choose a platter that will be just big enough for the full serving of snow peas.) Garnish with a tomato rose.
Serves 12.

JEAN-LOUIS PALLADIN'S PUMPKIN SOUP WITH PRESERVED DUCK HEARTS AND GIZZARDS

Giblets:
1 pound duck hearts
1 pound duck gizzards
8 ounces coarse sea salt
freshly ground black pepper
4 cups duck fat, liquid

Soup:
1 3-pound pumpkin, peeled and diced
1 medium pumpkin, top cut out and hollowed to serve the soup
1 medium onion, chopped
3 shallots, diced
2 cloves of garlic, peeled and diced
3 ounces ham (jambon de Bayonee or prosciutto) diced
1/2 cup diced carrot
1/2 cup diced leek
1 stalk celery, diced
1 small turnip, diced
2 medium potatoes, diced
2 branches fresh thyme (or 1/2 teaspoon dried)
1 bay leaf
5 cups consommé
Freshly ground black pepper

Giblets: Sprinkle the hearts and gizzards with the salt and some pepper. Let sit 1 hour or more, tossing occasionally. Cover with the duck grease and slowly simmer for 1 to 1 1/2 hours. Let cool in the fat.

Soup: Dice 2 cups of the pumpkin *very* finely to garnish the bowls. Blanch.

Cook everything except the consommé and the 2 cups very finely diced pumpkin in a large pan with a little of the duck fat. When it is all soft add the consommé and simmer slowly for 1 to 1 1/2 hours adding a little water if necessary. Blend it all together in a food processor until smooth. If you wish you can finish it with a little butter (3 to 4 ounces) or heavy cream.

Sprinkle some of the blanched, finely diced pumpkin in the soup bowls. Slice the hearts and gizzards and arrange in the bowls. Present the bowls and ladle the hot soup out of the hollow pumpkin.
Serves 12.

BURT GREENE'S PUMPKIN BURNT CREAM

3 cups whipping cream
1/2 cup granulated sugar
6 egg yolks
2/3 cup solid-pack pumpkin
1/4 teaspoon ground cinnamon
1/8 teaspoon ground ginger
Pinch of ground cloves
1 tablespoon dark rum
1/2 cup light brown sugar

Heat oven to 325°. Cook cream and granulated sugar in top of a double boiler, stirring frequently, over simmering water until sugar dissolves. Beat egg yolks in a large mixing bowl until light and fluffy; gradually whisk in pumpkin, cinnamon, ginger, cloves, and rum. Slowly stir in warm cream. Pour mixture into a 1-quart soufflé dish. Place dish in a roasting pan. Pour boiling water into pan to depth of 1 1/2 inches. Bake in the center of the oven until a knife inserted in the center of the custard comes out fairly clean, about 1 1/2 hours. Remove dish from pan; cool on a rack to room temperature. Refrigerate, covered, 6 hours or overnight.

Preheat broiler 15 minutes before serving. Sprinkle top of custard with brown sugar. Place dish in a pan; surround with ice. Place under broiler until sugar is melted and browned. Serve immediately.
Serves 6 to 8.

ABE DE LA HOUSSAYE'S CORN BREAD AND JALAPEÑO DRESSING

4 cups corn bread
3 tablespoons melted butter
5 jalapeño peppers, seeded and sliced (use gloves)
1 small onion, finely chopped
1 stalk celery, finely chopped
1 cup chicken stock or canned broth

Grind corn bread in food processor. Heat butter in sauté pan. Add jalapeños, onion, and celery. Cook 2 minutes. Add corn bread and stir well. Add stock, stir well, and cook 2 minutes.
Serves 4.

PERLA MEYERS' COINTREAU CRANBERRY PRESERVES

2 packages cranberries
3 Golden Delicious apples
1 cup fresh orange juice
1 cup raisins
2 teaspoons cinnamon
1 3/4 cups sugar
1/4 cup Cointreau
Grated rind of 2 oranges
Grated rind of 1 lemon

Peel, core, and cube the apples. Combine all of the ingredients except the Cointreau and cook until it is reduced to a preserve-like texture, about 45 minutes. Add the Cointreau. This can be kept for several weeks.
Serves 10 to 20.

LYDIE MARSHALL'S RAGOUT OF ONIONS, BACON, AND CHESTNUTS

20 small white onions
20 water-packed chestnuts
1/2 pound slab bacon in one piece
1 tablespoon olive oil
Salt to taste
Pepper to taste

Slice off the rind from the bacon and cut the meat in 2 or 3 pieces; cover with cold water and bring to a boil. Boil for 5 minutes. Drain and cut into 1/2-inch cubes. Heat oil in a skillet, sauté the bacon over medium heat until crisp, and remove the bacon with a slotted spoon. Set it aside. Sauté the onions in the bacon fat, tossing them once in a while until golden, about 15 minutes. Add the chestnuts, toss, and sauté for another 2 to 3 minutes. Add the bacon. Sprinkle salt and pepper to taste, cover, and continue cooking for another 15 minutes or so. Taste and correct seasoning.
Serves 6 to 8.

ANDRÉE'S-MEDITERRANEAN'S BABA GHANNOUSH

2 large eggplants, whole
1/2 cup tahini (crushed sesame paste)
1/2 cup water
1/4 cup olive oil
1/4 cup lemon juice
1 large clove garlic, crushed
Salt
Pepper
3 tablespoons Italian parsley, chopped

Puncture eggplants in several places and place under the broiler for about 45 minutes, turning on each side every 10 to 15 minutes. Broil until black and blistered. Ideally, broil it outdoors on a barbecue grill. Allow to cool and scrape eggplant from skin as close as possible without getting any of the charred particles. (This will impart a delicious smoky flavor.)

In a food processor or mixing bowl combine tahini, water, olive oil, and lemon juice. Add garlic, mixing until white. Season with salt and pepper to taste. Add eggplant and process in short on and off strokes until mixture is blended but still has some coarse texture and is not overly smooth. Stir in 2 tablespoons of the parsley and spoon into a serving dish. Sprinkle with remainder of parsley and serve.
Serves 10 to 20.

DIETER SCHORNER'S APPLE GRATINÉ WITH CRANBERRIES

Fruit Gratiné:
4 apples
4-6 tablespoons butter, melted
4 teaspoons honey
6-8 teaspoons cranberries

Armagnac Sauce:
1 egg yolk
1 teaspoon vanilla-sugar
1 tablespoon Armagnac
2 tablespoons whipped cream

Peel and slice apples. Place the sliced apples on a baking dish, brush with butter and honey, and bake in a 400° oven until brown and slightly soft. While the apples are baking, rinse the cranberries, cover with cold water, and cook until tender, about 5 minutes.

To make the Armagnac Sauce, beat the egg yolk and the sugar together. Add the Armagnac, then fold in the whipped cream.

Place the apples on a heat-proof serving dish, sprinkle with fresh-stewed cranberries on top, and drizzle one tablespoon of the Armagnac sauce on top of the fruit. Place under the broiler until golden brown.
Serves 4.

RICHARD LAVIN'S GRAVLAX

1 side salmon (about 3 pounds)
2 ounces sugar
2 ounces kosher salt
2 ounces coarse crushed black pepper
3 bunches dill (whole)
4 oranges, thinly sliced
4 red onions, thinly sliced

Vegetables Julienne:
2 red peppers
2 carrots
2 white turnips
3 bunches chives

Mustard Sauce:
2 tablespoons honey
2 tablespoons dijon mustard
3/4 cup crème fraiche
1 tablespoon chopped dill

Remove small bones from salmon with tweezers. Mix sugar, salt, and black pepper together; generously spread over both sides of fish. Place fish on large piece of cheesecloth. Cover each side of fish with dill first, then orange slices and onion slices. Cover and wrap in cheesecloth, place on pan, cover with another pan, and place in refrigerator with a 5-pound weight on top. Allow to cure 2 days, then drain off liquid. Remove dill and orange and onions; brush off cure. Slice thinly.

Slice the vegetables very thinly by hand or use a mandolin. Arrange the vegetables around the fish as a decorative accompaniment.

Mix together all of the ingredients for the mustard sauce. Serve on the side.
Serves 25.

JAMES BEARD'S QUINCE TART

Pastry:
2½ cups flour
½ pound unsalted butter, softened
2 tablespoons sugar
3 egg yolks
½ teaspoon cinnamon
Grated zest of 1 lemon

Filling:
6 large quince
3 cups water
3 cups sugar
Juice of 1 lemon, strained
1 stick cinnamon
2 whole cloves
2 tablespoons chopped almonds, roasted lightly

Place the flour in a large bowl. Make a well and add the butter, cut into small pieces, sugar, egg yokes, cinnamon, and lemon zest. Knead well until well mixed and the dough forms a ball. Chill until firm.

For the filling, peel and core the quince, saving the seeds. Cut the quince into julienne strips. Meanwhile, in a heavy skillet or enamel pan, boil together the water, sugar and lemon juice, then add the strips of quince along with the cinnamon, cloves, and quince seeds tied in a cheesecloth bag. The pectin in the seeds acts as a thickener. Bring the mixture to a boil, lower the heat, and simmer for 1½ hours, or until the juice is thickened. Stir the mixture from time to time, being careful that it doesn't stick or burn. Discard the bag and let the mixture cool.

Preheat the oven to 375°. Roll out two-thirds of the pastry between 2 pieces of wax paper and fit into a 12-inch round cake or quiche pan with a removable bottom. Bake for 10 minutes.

Fill the shell with the quince mixture and use the remaining pastry to make a lattice-work top. Place the tart in the oven and bake for 20 to 30 minutes or until the pastry is golden brown and the preserves are bubbling.

Remove the tart from the oven and sprinkle the almonds on top. Let cool at least 2 to 3 hours or overnight but do not refrigerate.

Serve with whipped cream, crème fraîche, sour cream, or vanilla ice cream.

Festive Crafts

99

Macy's Thanksgiving Book

TURKEY APPLIQUÉ

TURKEY APPLIQUÉ PILLOW

Materials Needed:
2 17" squares of quilted fabric
Scraps of calico and country print fabric
52" red rickrack
68" red piping
1 12-oz. bag polyester filling
Tracing paper
Soft lead pencil
Straight pins
Red thread

Take one 17" piece of fabric and machine sew the rickrack around the square 2" in from the sides. Make a pattern using the tracing paper and a soft lead pencil: trace the illustration in the book, cut out the picture leaving a rough border of about 1", then pin this to the appropriate pieces of cloth. For a turkey of all one color, keep the traced picture intact. For a patchwork turkey like the one shown, cut out each part separately. Pin the pieces of fabric that make up the turkey in place on the quilted fabric and inside the rickrack. Machine appliqué each piece one at a time, using the red thread. Go slowly.

Take the second 17" square of quilted fabric for the back of the pillow. Put the right side of the two pieces of quilted fabric together. Pin red piping in between the two. With the machine, baste the piping to the front and back of the pillow using a 1/2" seam. Then machine sew all the way around, leaving a 3" to 4" space. Turn the pillow right side out and stuff. Hand-stitch the pillow closed.

CORNUCOPIA WITH DRIED FLOWERS

Materials Needed:
Cornucopia basket
Scissors or wire cutters
Florist's foam, 9" × 3"
4 stems dried leaves
Approximately 50 assorted dried flowers (for the arrangement pictured, use German statice, dyed wheat, bleached teasle, florentine, and dried leaves)
Kitchen knife

Carve the foam with the kitchen knife to fit into the small end of the cornucopia basket. Try to carve it for as secure a fit as possible. Place the cornucopia on the surface where it will be displayed. Strew the leaves on the bottom, then begin arranging the dried flowers and stalks. Build up the arrangement from the bottom, placing the larger stalks in first, then the smaller. Cut the everlastings as you need to, to vary the lengths. To make the arrangement, push the stems into the foam firmly but gently. (You may want to arrange the flowers loosely in the cornucopia first, before putting the foam inside.)

WHEAT BASKET CENTERPIECE

Materials Needed:
Low basket with handle
About 30 stalks of wheat
About 30 strands of florist's raffia
Miniature fruits to fill the basket (clementines, mandarin oranges, lady apples, fiorello pears are all good choices)
Scissors or sharp knife

Soak wheat in hot water for 10 minutes before using, to make it more pliable. Start with one strand of wheat at one end of the basket handle. With the top of the wheat facing downward, cover handle with stem, moving to the other side of the basket handle. Cut off excess. Then wrap the wheat securely to the handle with the raffia. Tie the raffia at either end in a square knot. Continue this process until the wheat fans across the handle. Cover all exposed parts with the raffia. Arrange the fruits in the basket.

Macy's Thanksgiving Book

Festive Crafts

CHILDREN'S PLACE SETTING

Materials Needed:

FOR THE PLACEMAT—

2 blue plastic mats, approximately 12 3/4" x 16 3/4" and 1 each of red, yellow, and white
Tracing paper
Crafts glue
Scissors
Red embroidery thread
Embroidery needle
Black thread
Standard needle
Straight pins

FOR THE NAPKIN—

1 piece of red fabric 17" x 17"
Blue embroidery thread

FOR THE NAME CARD—

1 piece of stiff paper, 4" x 6"
1 piece of blue mat, 4" x 3"
Red embroidery thread

Trace the illustration of Woody's head onto the tracing paper. Cut out, leaving a rough border of approximately 1/2" to 3/4" and pin to a red mat. Cut the pattern out of the red mat and glue it on the lower right side of one of the blue mats 1" from the bottom and side edges. Using yellow for the mouth, white for eyeballs, and blue for the irises; repeat the pattern process or draw the details freehand on the colored mats. Glue these details lightly to the red head. When dry, stitch everything in place with black thread. To make the mat's border, use an "X" stitch (see illustration) with the red embroidery thread, all the way around the periphery of the blue mat.

For the napkin, fold the fabric's edges under 1/8" all the way around and "X" stitch the border with the blue thread.

Fold the stiff paper in half lengthwise to begin work on the name card. Glue the blue plastic lightly to the paper and "X" stitch around the paper 1/2" in from the edge the whole way around.

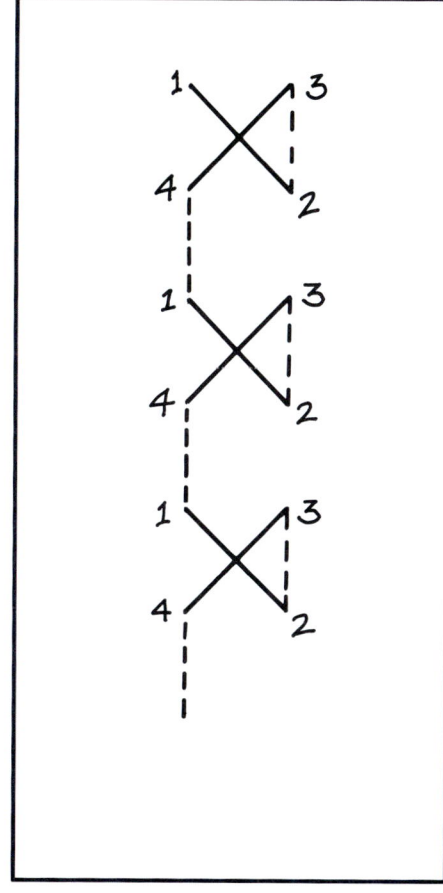

FLOAT CENTERPIECE

Materials Needed:

Styrofoam rectangle, approximately 11 1/2" x 7" x 2"
Small tubes of purple, blue, and green acrylic paint
4 round jar lids, 3" x 1/4"
Gold enamel spray paint
3 round and 3 heart-shaped air-filled balloons on sticks, about 7"
Various colors construction paper
3 yds. each of gold, green, and red paper ribbon
Scissors
Paintbrush
Crafts glue
Cement glue

Paint the styrofoam block blue with the acrylic paint. Spray the jar lids with the gold enamel paint. Let both dry at least 1 hour. Using the cement glue, attach the wheels to the styrofoam, 1" in from the ends. Press hard for a few minutes for the glue to set, then let dry.

Paint one side of the 3 round balloons with acrylic paint—blue, purple, and green. Cut 1"-wide strips the whole length of the construction paper and curl by running the paper against the inner edge of the scissor blade. Curl ribbon the same way. Arrange the paper and ribbon to your liking and attach to the center of the round balloons using the crafts glue (see photograph). Cut the straws so the balloons are at various heights. Press the straws into the top of the foam. Add more ribbon and paper to the top and back side of the float.

POMANDER BALLS

Materials Needed:
1 orange
1 apple
1 fairly ripe pear
6 oz. cloves
1 oz. orris root
2 tbsp. cinnamon
Small nail
1½ yds. of 1½" white lace
1 yd. each of 2 different colors of ½" ribbon
1 piece of netting, 15" × 15"
12" satin ribbon

Cover the fruit completely with cloves, about 2 oz. for each fruit. You can press the cloves directly into the apple and pear; but for the orange, use the nail to puncture the orange rind before pushing in the cloves. When this is done, roll the fruit in the orris root mixed with cinnamon. The orris root acts as a preservative and the cinnamon adds fragrance. Brush off the excess orris root and place the fruit in an airy, warm, dry spot for 3 to 4 weeks. The fruit will shrivel slightly. When dry, tie a ribbon around the orange, a piece of lace about the apple, and the netting around the pear. Hang the fruit or display it in a bowl.

Festive Crafts

POTPOURRI GOURDS

Materials Needed:
Small dried ornamental gourds (the ones illustrated are a warty gourd and a star gourd)
Crafts knife
Fine sandpaper
Clear acrylic spray paint
Kitchen knife or steel wool pad without soap
Pen
Potpourri

Make sure the gourds are thoroughly dried. Carefully scrape away any encrusted dirt or other extraneous matter with a kitchen knife or steel wool pad or both. Rinse under running water. Let dry for at least 1/2 hour.

Draw a cutting line (see illustration) with the pen across the center for the warty gourd or around the points for the star gourd. Make an incision and cut around the gourd with the crafts knife. Don't press too hard because the walls are thin and you may collapse the gourd. When open, clean the interior of the gourd; scrape out the seeds and flesh, then rinse under water. Let dry for an hour.

Sand the interior and exterior of the gourds, including the rims, with the sandpaper. Apply 2 to 3 coats of the spray paint inside and out. This will strengthen the gourds and enhance their color.

Place your favorite potpourri inside and set out on a side table or in the bathroom.

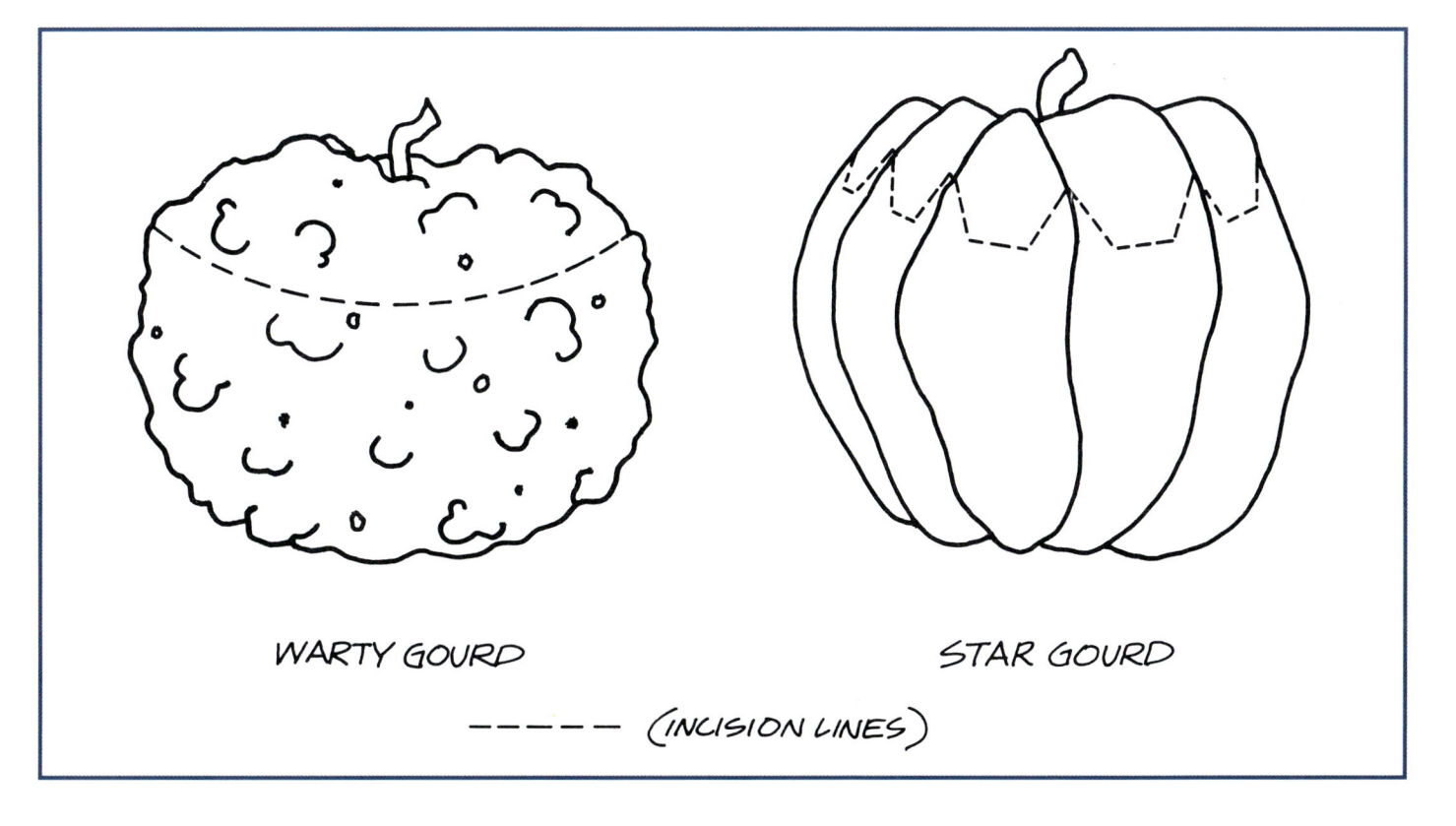

WARTY GOURD   STAR GOURD

----- (INCISION LINES)

Boys Collar

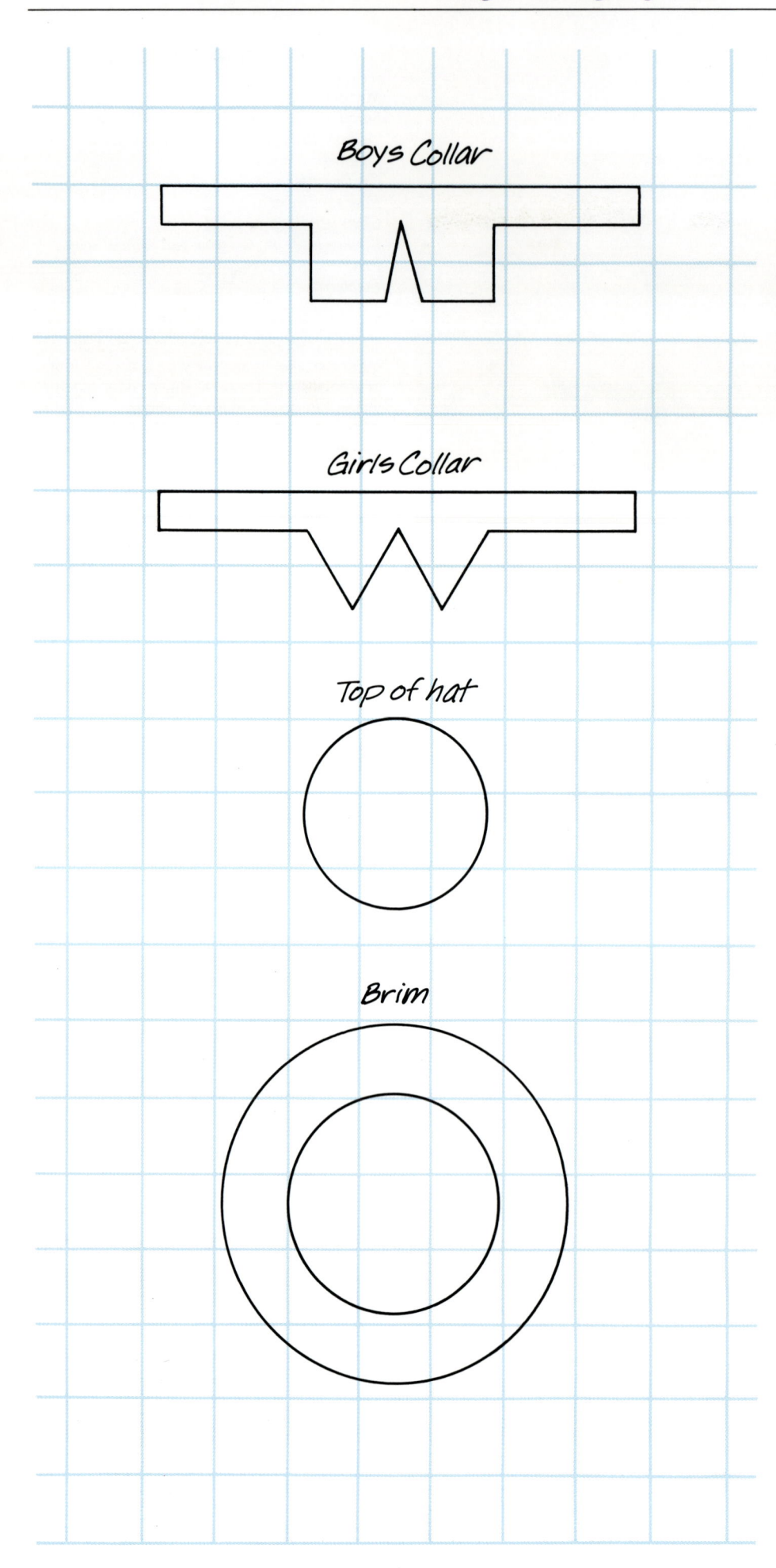

Girls Collar

Top of hat

Brim

PILGRIM DOLLS

Materials Needed:
2 12" tubes from aluminum foil, wax paper, etc.
2 styrofoam balls
Crafts glue
Embroidery needle
Embroidery thread
2 flesh-colored socks
FOR THE GIRL—
1 piece of stiff white paper
3 buttons
1 17" square of brown felt
Yarn (for hair)
Ribbon (for bows)
1 17" square of white felt (for bandanna, skirt, and collar)
Scraps of brown or blue felt (for eyes) and red and pink (for mouth and cheeks)
FOR THE BOY—
1 17" square of brown felt
1 17" square yellow felt
Scraps of black felt (for the eyes and hat and belt buckles) and red felt (for the mouth and cheeks)
Yarn (for hair)
1 7-oz. paper cup

Glue the styrofoam ball to the tube. Let dry 1 hour. Cover the entire ball and tube with the sock, fitting the toe of the sock to the ball, the heel toward the back of the tube, and the remainder into the bottom of the tube.

Girl: Sew the brown felt up the back of the tube. Sew collar in the back to the very top of the tube. Take stiff white paper and place the white felt over it. Sew ends to curve it to the body of the doll. This will make the apron stick out. Sew 3 buttons about 1/2" apart down the front of the dress. Braid yarn. Sew to the top of the head as pictured. Tie bows on the ends of the braids. Sew the triangle of white felt to the head (as pictured) for the bandanna; two points should be tacked on to either side of the head, the third point to the back of the head. Glue on felt details for eyes, mouth, and cheeks. Embroider eyelashes and eyebrows.

Boy: Sew clothes, belt, and collar in the same way as for the girl. Glue the black felt buckle on the belt. Follow the directions for the girl to make the face. Sew hair on top of the head. For the hat, cut the paper cup so it is only 1 1/2" high. Glue a piece of brown felt onto it. Trace around the top of the covered cup onto the felt, then draw another circle around the traced circle 1" larger than the first. Cut this circular strip, then sew it around the inside edge to the top of the cup as a brim. Next trace the bottom of the cup onto the felt, then cut this circle out. Sew it to the bottom of the cup. Place the hat securely on the doll's head, tacking it in a few places with a needle and thread to keep it in place.

Festive Crafts

DECORATED CANDLE

Materials Needed:
2 red candles, 3" x 9"
Assorted dried beans and seeds: 1/4 c. lentils, 1/4 c. split peas, 1/2 c. black beans, 1/2 c. pumpkin seeds
Crafts glue
Small paint brush

To make the candle illustrated in the photo above, gather around the diameter. Press on the first row of black beans. Let dry 1 hour. Brush on another line of glue and press on a row of pumpkin seeds. Repeat this process using lentils, split peas, then black beans again.

WHEAT MOTIF

WHEAT PLACEMATS

Materials Needed:
Oval-shaped straw mat, 18½" × 12"
Brown enamel spray paint
Gold enamel paint
1 sheet of stencil or stiff paper
Crafts knife or razor blade
Chalk
No. 2 stencil brush
Turpentine
FOR THE NAPKIN RING—
Wooden ring, 5½" x 1¼"

Spray mat with brown paint. Apply 2 to 3 coats, allowing each coat to dry at least 1 hour. Set aside. Using the illustration provided, draw or trace the wheat motif onto the stiff paper. Cut out the pattern exactly with the crafts knife or razor blade, taking great care; this will be your stencil. Now, using chalk as your marker, measure 1½" in from the edge of the mat, all the way around. This will be your guide as you place the stencil around the mat. Lining up the stencil to the chalk line, tape the stencil to the mat. Carefully fill in the area with the gold paint; hold the brush straight up in the air—perpendicular to the mat—and take small up-and-down strokes. Again, be very careful as you remove the stencil. Repeat this process, leaving about ¼" between each pattern as you work your way around the mat edge. If your hand is not that steady, you may prefer to let the first stenciled motif dry—about 1 hour—before you go on to the next one.

The process is very similar for the napkin rings. Since you already have your stencil, you can tape it directly onto the wooden ring. Do make sure that the paint on the stencil is dry and will not leave stray marks on the napkin ring. Using the same strokes, fill in the stencil. One pattern should suffice for the napkin ring, as shown.

A Thanksgiving Anthology

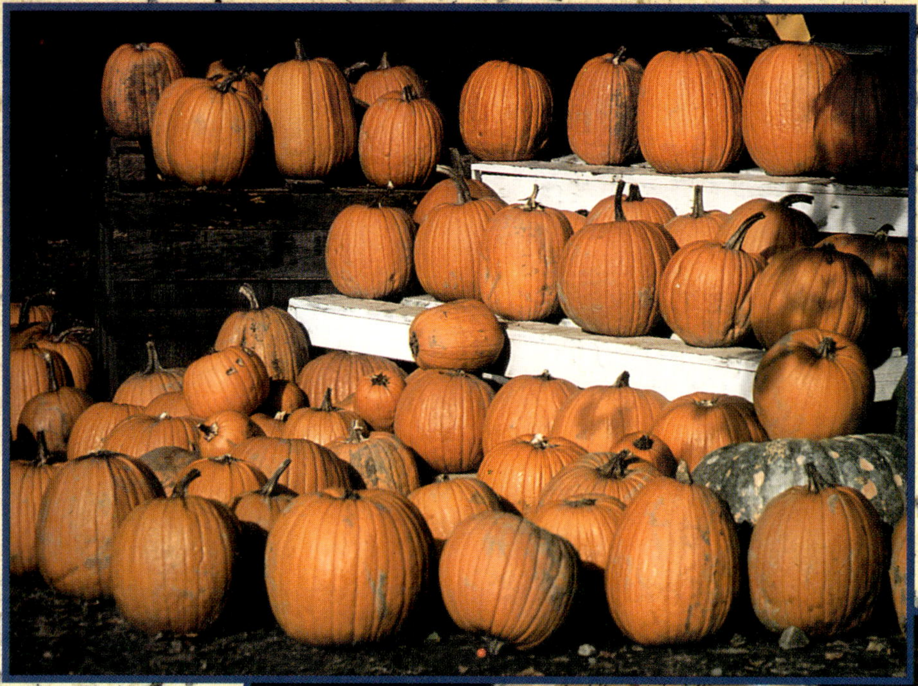

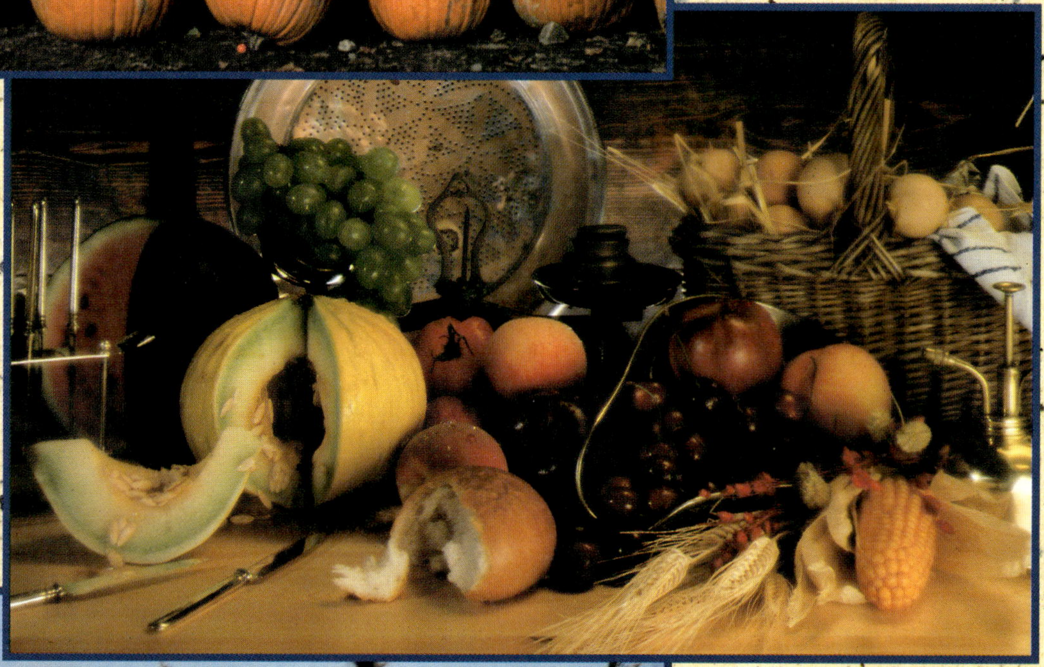

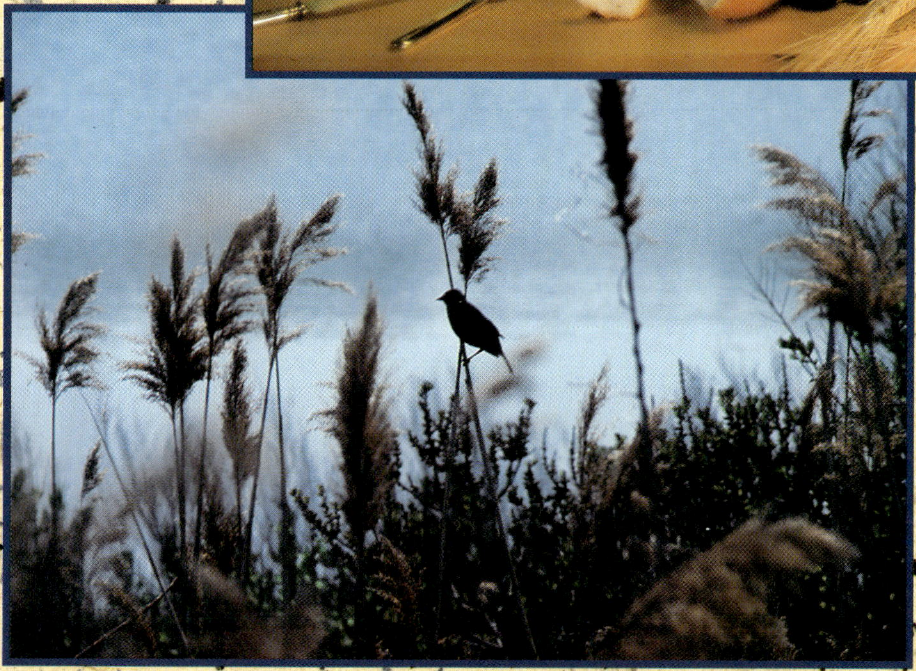

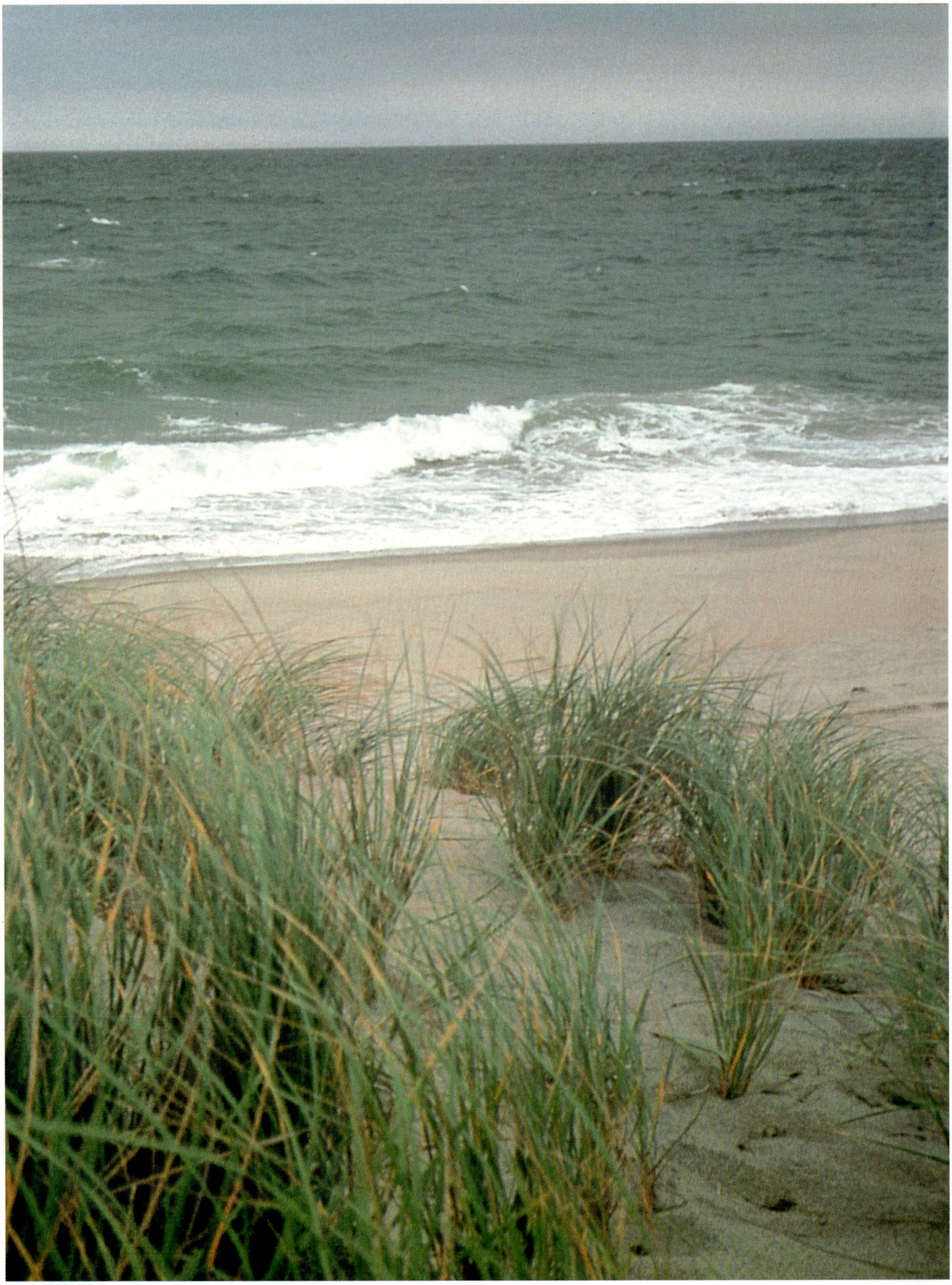

America the Beautiful

Katherine Lee Bates
Samuel A. Ward

O beau-ti-ful for spa-cious skies, For am-ber waves of grain, For pur-ple moun-tain ma-jes-ties A-bove the fruit-ed plain! A-mer-i-ca! A-mer-i-ca! God shed His grace on thee, And crown thy good with broth-er-hood From sea to shin-ing sea!

2. O beautiful for pilgrim feet,
   Whose stern impassion'd stress,
   A thoroughfare for freedom beat
   Across the wilderness!
   America! America!
   God mend thine every flaw,
   Confirm thy soul in self control,
   Thy liberty in law!

3. O beautiful for glorious tale
   Of liberating strife,
   When valiantly for man's avail,
   Men lavished precious life!
   America! America!
   May God thy gold refine,
   Till all success be nobleness,
   And ev'ry gain divine!

4. O beautiful for patriot dream
   That sees beyond the years
   Thine alabaster cities gleam
   Undimmed by human tears!
   America! America!
   God shed His grace on thee,
   And crown thy good with brotherhood
   From sea to shining sea!

The Landing of the Pilgrim Fathers

The breaking waves dashed high
    On a stern and rock-bound coast,
And the woods against a stormy sky
    Their giant branches tossed;

And the heavy night hung dark
    The hills and waters o'er,
When a band of exiles moored their bark
    On the wild New England shore.

Not as the conqueror comes,
    They, the true-hearted, came;
Not with the roll of the stirring drums,
    And the trumpet that sings of fame:

Not as the flying come,
    In silence and in fear;
They shook the depths of the desert gloom
    With their hymns of lofty cheer.

Amidst the storm they sang,
    And the stars heard, and the sea;
And the sounding aisles of the dim woods rang
    To the anthem of the free.

The ocean eagle soared
    From his nest by the white wave's foam,
And the rocking pines of the forest roared,—
    This was their welcome home.

There were men with hoary hair
    Amidst that pilgrim-band:
Why had they come to wither there,
    Away from their childhood's land?

There was woman's fearless eye,
    Lit by her deep love's truth;
There was manhood's brow serenely high,
    And the fiery heart of youth.

What sought they thus afar?
    Bright jewels of the mine?
The wealth of seas, the spoils of war?—
    They sought a faith's pure shrine!

Ay, call it holy ground,
    The soil where first they trod;
They have left unstained what there they found,—
    Freedom to worship God.

—Felicia D. Hemans

Giving Thanks

For the hay and the corn and the wheat that
    is reaped,
For the labor well done, and the barns that
    are heaped,
For the sun and the dew and the sweet
    honeycomb,
For the rose and the song, and the harvest
    brought home—
    Thanksgiving! Thanksgiving!

For the trade and the kill and the wealth in
    our land,
For the cunning and strength of the
    workingman's hand,
For the good that our artists and poets have
    taught,
For the friendship that hope and affection
    have brought—
    Thanksgiving! Thanksgiving!

For the homes that with purest affection are
    blest,
For the season of plenty and well-deserved
    rest,
For our country extending from sea unto sea;
The land that is known as the "Land of the
    Free"—
    Thanksgiving! Thanksgiving!

        —Anonymous

Thanksgiving

In a valley far from the noisy town,
The old farm-house stands low and brown.

Year by year has the summer sun
And the winter storm its work well done,

Till from door-stone broad to roof-tree high
It seems a relic of days gone by.

Patches of moss on the shingles grow,
Last year's nests in the porch below;

Swallows build in the chimney wide;
Lilac bushes grow just outside;

Their clusters of purplish blossoms fair,
Filling with perfume the soft spring air.

Bearded grain, and tasseled corn,
Wave in the breath of each summer morn;

While the ripened apples softly fall
In autumn days by the orchard wall.

Children's voices are heard no more
Happy at play by the kitchen door.

One by one they have grown, and gone,
And the old folks now are left alone,

With figures bent, and whitened hair,
And wrinkled faces that once were fair:

Eyes needing spectacles to see,
And steps not spry as they used to be.

Bound by the ties that hold the heart
Of the old brown house they seem a part.

* * * * * *

Knitting in hand in her rocking-chair,
"Mother" muses on days that were.

Every click of the shining steel,
As she sets the seam, or binds the heel,

Takes up the stitches thick and fast,
In the golden web of the days long past.

She sees in the orchard a tiny mound,
Level now with the earth around:

Her one wee daughter, sweet and fair,
She laid to rest under daisies there;

Fifty years! but it seems a day—
Living, she too had been old and gray.

Her memory lives, as in those young days,
"The baby" with pretty, winsome ways.

A tear-drop gathers and dims her sight,
And falls unseen on the needles bright.

* * * * * *

"Father" dozes o'er paper or book,
Smoking his pipe in the chimney nook;

With a frequent glance at the swaying chair,
To be sure that mother is resting there.

Reading the news by his own fireside,
He scarcely dreams that the world's so wide.

He has sent his sons to do their part
In the money-getting busy mart:

Four stalwart men, and he thinks with pride
There were no such boys in the country side.

He lives in them again to-day,
Since his youth and strength have passed away.

Oh, the golden heart-warming autumn days!
The air is full of a dreamy haze:

So quiet the noisy brooklets seem,
We hear their dashing as in a dream.

The sloping hill-sides, and mountains grand,
In a glaze of glory gorgeous stand,

Red, and yellow, and golden brown,
A mass of color fluttering down:

Hues that an artist ne'er can trace—
Nature's own for October days.

Load by load the fragrant hay
Has been gathered in and stowed away;

Wheat, rye, oats, a goodly store,
Bundled and thrashed on the broad barn floor;

Big golden pumpkins piled up high
For the winter's feed, and the luscious pie;

Bins in the cellar, filled with care,
Spitzenberg, greening, and russet rare;

New sweet cider sipped through a straw—
Nectar fit for the gods to draw.

* * * * * *

There's a dream of snow in the frosty air;
The skies are gray, and the fields are bare;

The whistling wind, as it creeps around,
Has a sort of sorrowful sighing sound.

Boughs of green, that have filled up high
The fireplace in summer days gone by,

Are cast aside; and morn and night,
The hearth-fire blazes warm and bright.

There's bustle and stir at the old home farm:
Some potent spell works its magic charm.

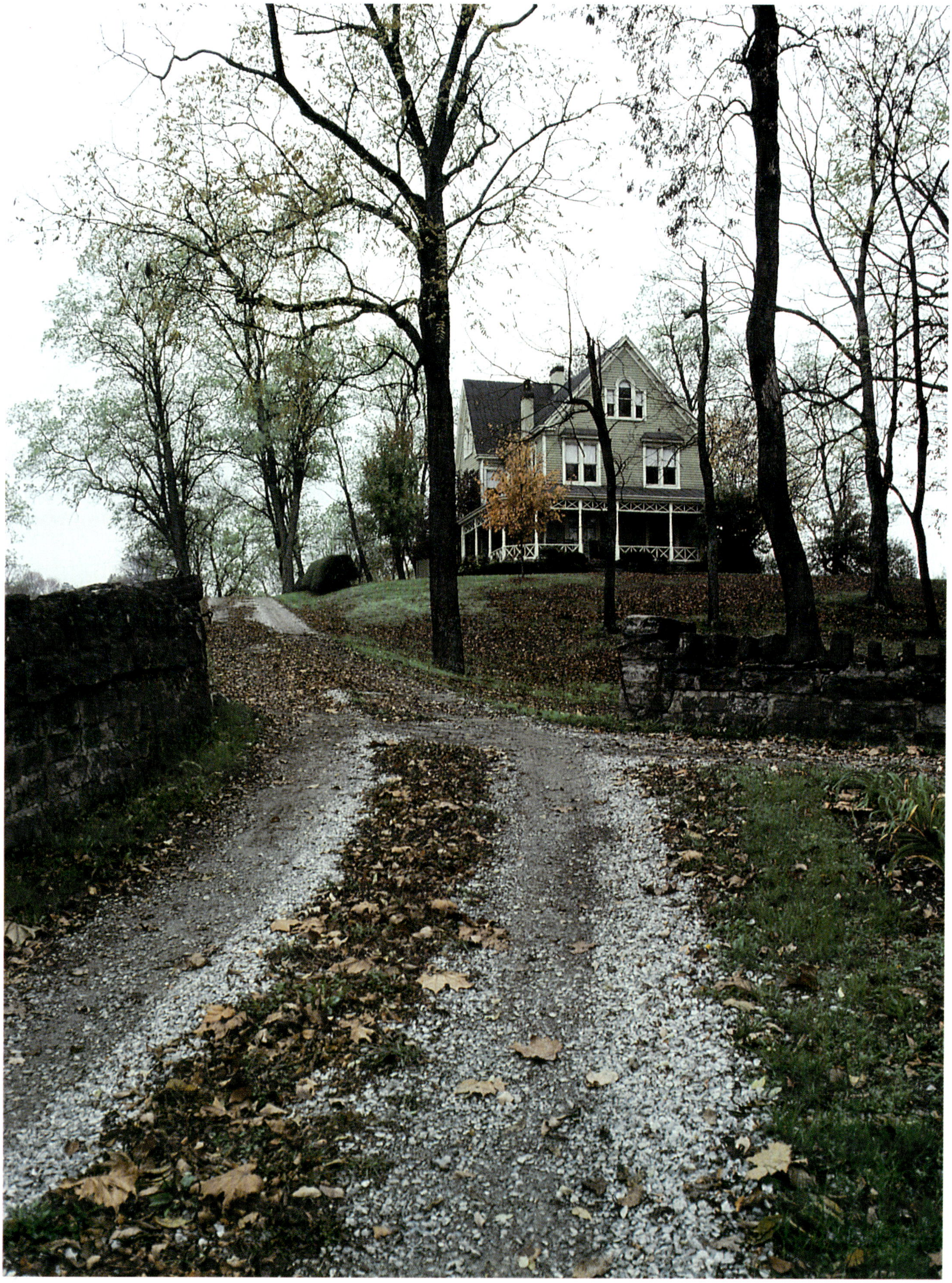

From cellar to garret a sense of cheer
Pervades the home-like atmosphere.

The very smoke curls in joyous rings,
And leaps to its airy wanderings.

Savory odors float from afar,
When the oven door is left ajar;

And the cupboard shelves are loaded down
With flaky pies of a golden brown.

The fire burns bright in the "keeping-room."
Chambers above are all aboom

With "feathered star," and "rising sun,"
"Job's trouble," "diamond," and
"herring-bone."

Works of art, tho' they be less fair
Than picture fine, or sculpture rare.

In the front porch oft does "mother" stand,
Shading her eyes with her withered hand;

Anxiously watching the lowering sky,
Where sullen clouds scud swiftly by;

Shutting the door, and saying low,
"I'm afraid we're bound to have some snow."

"Father" comes in from out of doors—
He's "done the milkin'," and "seen to the chores;"

He rubs his hands at the blaze so bright—
"I'm afeard it'll be a teejus night;

"But the cattle are housed, and the comin' storm
Will find all tidy, and snug, and warm.

"I sort o' hope we won't have snow;
It don't hardly seem as it could be so—

"That to-morrow Thanksgivin' Day will come,
And all the children are comin' home."

Yes! back once more to the old fireside—
Isaiah the eldest—his father' pride,

A middle-aged man with grayish hair,
And a face that shows some lines of care.

A banker—rich—they always stand
A little in awe of his wife so grand:

She isn't used to their country way,
And simple manners of every day.

Stephen too, with his gentle bride—
His parish is in the country side.

'Twas a happy day when his mother heard
His preaching of the Holy Word

From the old church pulpit perched so high—
His boyish wonder in days gone by.

Tho' the others are loved, and ne'er forgot,
In her heart he has always the warmest spot.

Captain William, their sailor boy—
How he used to shout his "Ship ahoy!"

In his dreams, and wake them all from sleep—
His home is now on the restless deep;

But his ship is in; he'll anchor lay,
To keep with them Thanksgiving Day.

And noisy Robert, full of glee,
As a college boy will ever be:

The youngsters think it a lucky day
When "Uncle Bob" will lead their play.

They're sure to have the best of fun,—
Mother hopes they're coming, every one.

Such bunches of dill and caraway,
Such huge seed cookies find their way

To little hands from her pockets deep,
Are secrets grandma alone can keep.

On the earth's broad bosom, bare and brown,
The snow falls softly, lightly down;

Tossed by the wind, in many a whirl
The feathery flakelets creep and curl;

Drape the boughs of the forest pine
In many a graceful pendulous line,

And seem in their purity to cling
Like a benison to everything.

But if all without is bleak and drear,
Within is comfort and happy cheer.

The huge fire logs in the chimney wide
Crackle and blaze as in gleeful pride.

Spread for the feast the table stands,
The work of cunning and skillful hands.

Ye lovers of ceramics draw near;
A tempting treasure waits you here.

Faience, Wedgwood, and Dresden fine,
Lowestoft, Canton, may all combine.

No such gems 'mong them all I see,
As in "mother's" best set of mulberry.

Only on state occasions rare
Is ever displayed this service fair:

It was "father's" gift on her wedding-day—
Not a piece broken or given away.

She looks with pride on the purplish bands,
Wipes a speck of dust with her wrinkled hands,

And hopes that "Isaiah's wife will see
Her table's as nice as need to be."

* * * * * *

Who shall picture the tempting array
Of dainties that graced the board that day?

Who can forget the frolic and fun
That followed when the meal was done?

Games for the youngsters of maddest glee,
Uncle Bob leading the revelry;

While the old folks talked in the fire-light's glow
Of other Thanksgivings they used to know.

All at home! not a single one
From the happy circle lost or gone.

When another year shall bring this day,
Father and mother, passed away,

Their life-work done, keep hand in hand
Their harvest home in a better land.

But the children visit the well-known spot—
The old brown house is not quite forgot.

And children's children hear them tell
Of the old home days they loved so well.

Over all the land in East and West,
All that is purest, noblest, best,

Throbs in the hearts that warmly glow
With thoughts of Thanksgivings long ago:

And memory's magnet links the chain
That draws each wanderer home again.

—BESSIE LAWRENCE

Come, Ye Thankful People, Come

St. George's Windsor G. J. Elrey

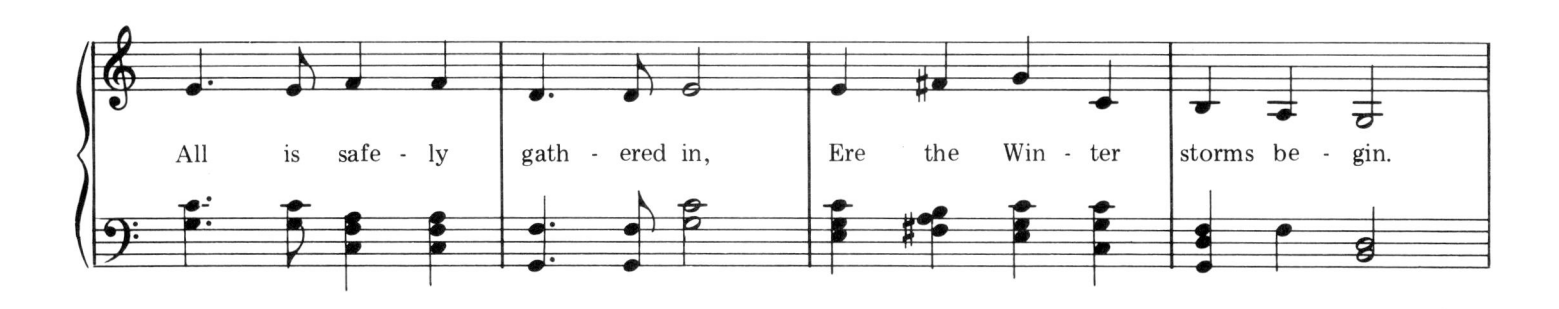

[Musical score with lyrics:]

Come ye thank-ful peo-ple come, Raise the song of har-vest home;
All is safe-ly gath-ered in, Ere the Win-ter storms be-gin.
God, our Mak-er doth pro-vide For our wants to be sup-plied:
Come to God's own tem-ple come, Raise the song of har-vest home A-men.

2. All the world is God's own field,
   Fruit unto His praise to yield;
   Wheat and fares together sown,
   Unto joy or sorrow grown;
   First the blade, and then the ear,
   Then the full corn shall appear;
   Lord of harvest, grant that we,
   Whole-some grain and pure may be.

3. For the Lord our God shall come,
   And shall take His harvest home;
   From His field shall in that day,
   All offenses purge away;
   Give His angels charge at last,
   In the five the fares to cast,
   But the fruitful ears to store,
   In His garner ever more.

4. Even so, Lord, quickly come,
   To thy final harvest home;
   Gather then thy people in,
   Free from sorrow, free from sin;
   There, forever purified,
   In thy presence to abide;
   Come with all thine angels come,
   Raise the glorious harvest home.

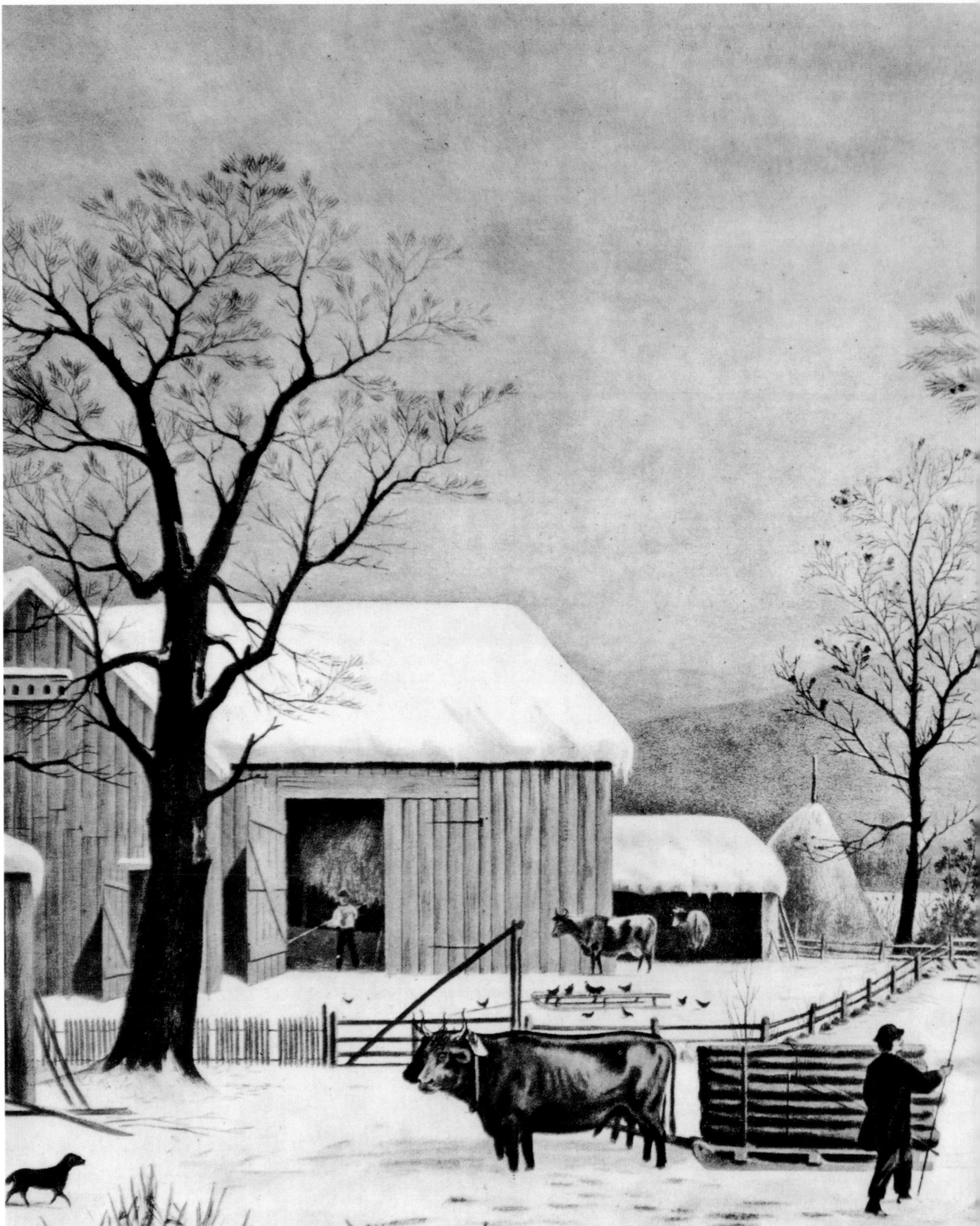

Over The River

Over the river and through the woods
To Grandmother's house we go;
The horse knows the way
To carry the sleigh
Through the white and drifting snow.

Over the river and through the woods,
Oh, how the wind does blow!
It stings the toes
And bites the nose,
As over the ground we go.

Over the river and through the woods
Trot fast, my dapple gray!
Spring over the ground
Like a hunting hound!
For this is Thanksgiving Day.

Over the river and through the woods,
To have a first-rate play.
Hear the bells ring,
Ting-a-ling-ding!
Hurrah for Thanksgiving Day!

Over the river and through the wood,
And straight through the barnyard gate.
We seem to go
Extremely slow—
It is so hard to wait!

Over the river and through the wood—
Now Grandfather's cap I spy!
Hurrah for the fun!
Is the turkey done?
Hurrah for the pumpkin pie!

—TRADITIONAL

Let Us Break Bread Together

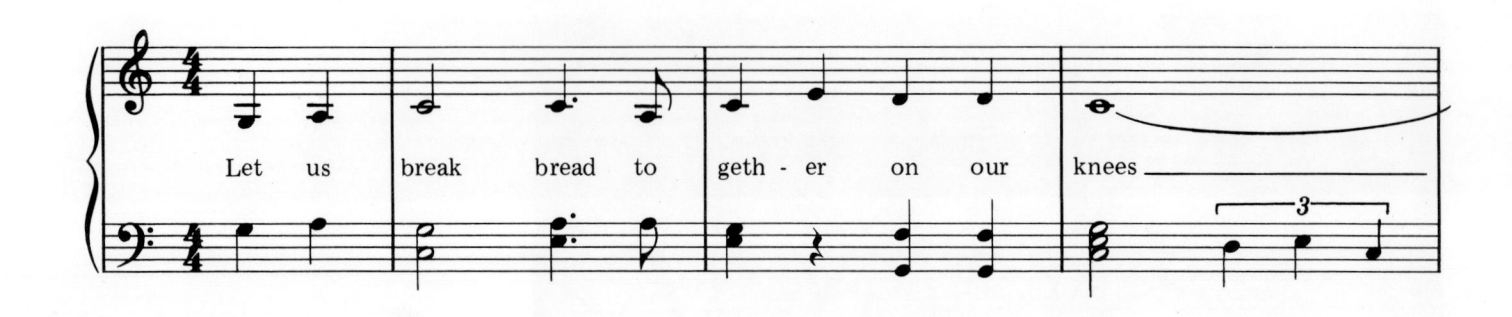

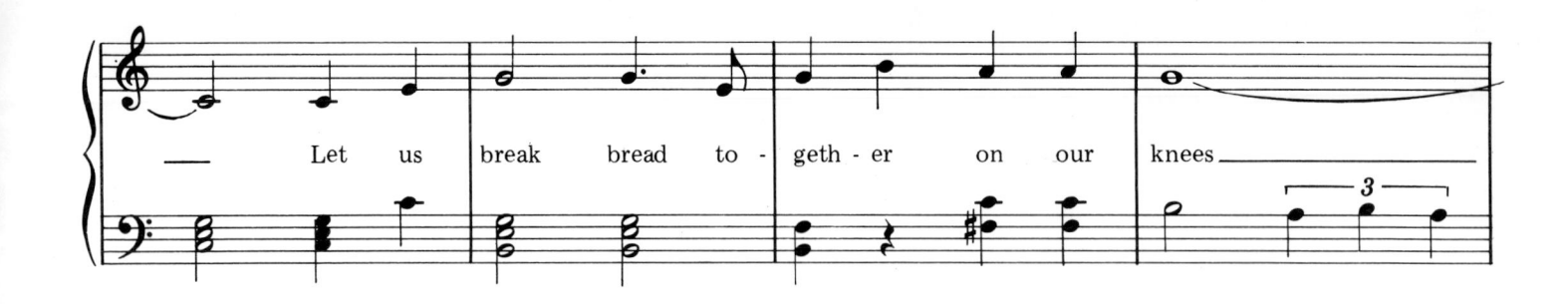

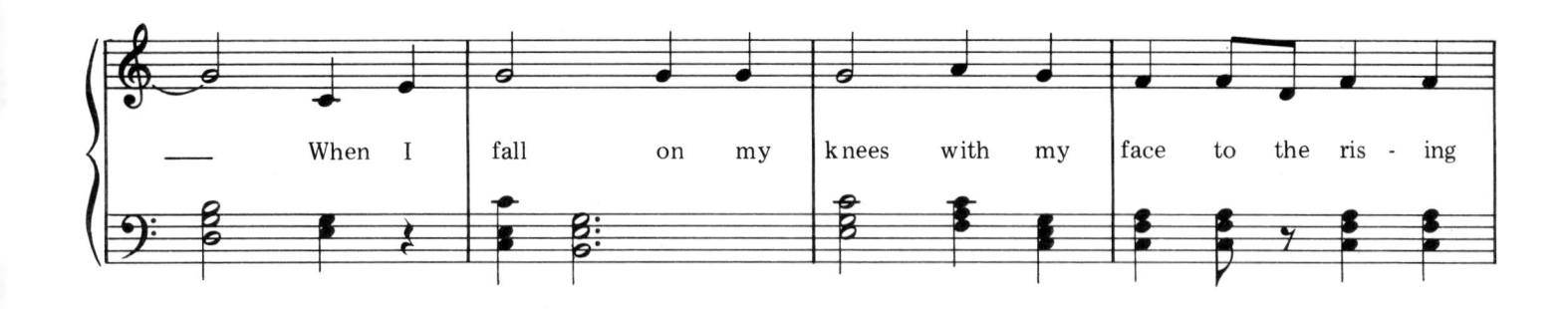

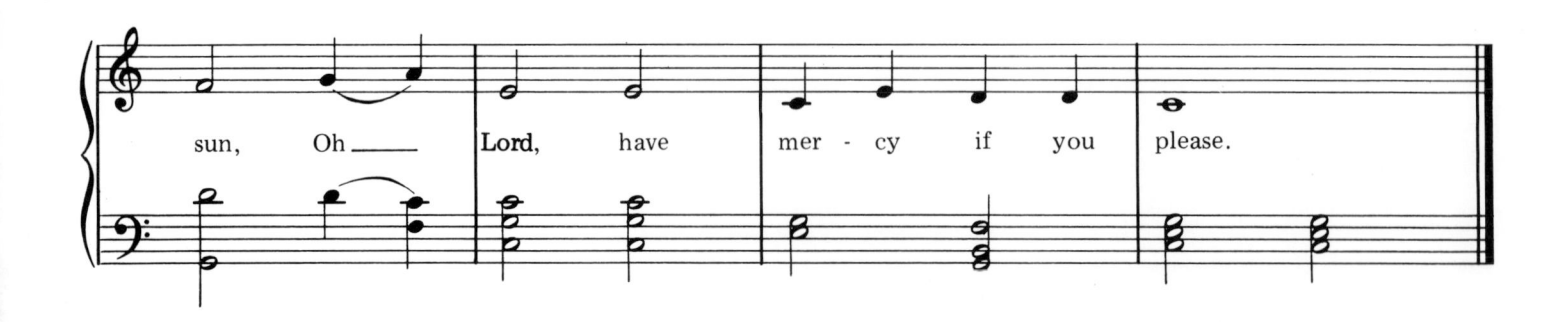

2. Let us drink wine together . . .
3. Let us all sing together . . .

A Thanksgiving Anthology

FROM *An Old-Fashioned Thanksgiving*

By Louisa May Alcott

Many years ago, up among the New Hampshire hills, lived Farmer Bassett, with a house full of sturdy sons and daughters growing up about him. They were poor in money, but rich in land and love, for the wide acres of wood, corn, and pasture land fed, warmed, and clothed the flock, while mutual patience, affection, and courage made the old farmhouse a very happy home.

November had come; the crops were in, and barn, buttery, and bin were overflowing with the harvest that rewarded the summer's hard work. The big kitchen was a jolly place just now, for in the great fire-place roared a cheerful fire; on the walls hung garlands of dried apples, onions, and corn; up aloft from the beams shone crook-necked squashes, juicy hams, and dried venison—for in those days deer still haunted the deep forests, and hunters flourished. Savory smells were in the air; on the crane hung steaming kettles, and down among the red embers copper sauce-pans simmered, all suggestive of some approaching feast.

A white-headed baby lay in the old blue cradle that had rocked seven other babies, now and then lifting his head to look out, like a round, full moon, then subsided to kick and crow contentedly, and suck the rosy apple he had no teeth to bite. Two small boys sat on the wooden settle shelling corn for popping, and picking out the biggest nuts from the goodly store their own hands had gathered in October. Four young girls stood at the long dresser, busily chopping meat, pounding spice, and slicing apples; and the tongues of Tilly, Prue, Roxy, and Rhody went as fast as their hands. Farmer Bassett, and Eph, the oldest boy, were ''chorin' 'round'' outside, for Thanksgiving was at hand, and all must be in order for that time-honored day.

To and fro, from table to hearth, bustled buxom Mrs. Bassett, flushed and floury, but busy and blithe as the queen bee of this busy little hive should be.

''I do like to begin seasonable and have things to my mind. Thanksgivin' dinners can't be drove, and it does take a sight of victuals to fill all these hungry stomicks,'' said the good woman, as she gave a vigorous stir to the great kettle of cider apple-sauce, and cast a glance of housewifely pride at the fine array of pies set forth on the buttery shelves.

Only one more day and then it will be time to eat. I didn't take but one bowl of hasty pudding this morning, so I shall have plenty of room when the nice things come,'' confided Seth to Sol, as he cracked a large hazel-nut as easily as a squirrel.

''No need of my starvin' beforehand. *I always* have room enough, and I'd like to have Thanksgiving every day,'' answered Solomon, gloating like a young ogre over the little pig that lay near by, ready for roasting.

''Sakes alive, I don't, boys! It's a marcy it don't come but once a year. I should be worn to a thread-paper with all this extra work atop of my winter weavin' and spinnin','' laughed their mother as she plunged her plump arms into the long bread-trough and began to knead the dough as if a famine was at hand.

Tilly, the oldest girl, a red-cheeked, black-eyed lass of fourteen, was grinding briskly at the mortar, for spices were costly, and not a grain must be wasted. Prue kept time with the chopper, and the twins sliced away at the apples till their little brown arms ached, for all knew how to work, and did so now with a will.

''I think it's real fun to have Thanksgiving at home. I'm sorry Gran'ma is sick, so we can't go there as usual, but I like to mess 'round here, don't you, girls?'' asked Tilly, pausing to take sniff at the spicy pestle.

''It will be kind of lonesome with only

124

A Thanksgiving Anthology

our own folks." "I like to see all the cousins and aunts, and have games, and sing," cried the twins, who were regular little romps, and could run, swim, coast, and shout as well as their brothers.

"I don't care a mite for all that. It will be so nice to eat dinner together, warm and comfortable at home," said quiet Prue, who loved her own cozy nooks like a cat.

"Come, girls, fly 'round and get your chores done, so we can clear away for dinner jest as soon as I clap my bread into the oven," called Mrs. Bassett presently, as she rounded off the last loaf of brown bread which was to feed the hungry mouths that seldom tasted any other.

"Here's a man comin' up the hill lively!" "Guess it's Gad Hopkins. Pa told him to bring a dezzen oranges, if they warn't too high!" shouted Sol and Seth, running to the door, while the girls smacked their lips at the thought of this rare treat, and Baby threw his apple overboard, as if getting ready for a new cargo.

But all were doomed to disappointment, for it was not Gad, with the much-desired fruit. It was a stranger, who threw himself off his horse and hurried up to Mr. Bassett in the yard, with some brief message that made the farmer drop his ax and look so sober that his wife guessed at once some bad news had come; and crying, "Mother's wuss! I know she is!" out ran the good woman, forgetful of the flour on her arms and the oven waiting for its most important batch.

The man said old Mr. Chadwick, down to Keene, stopped him as he passed, and told him to tell Mrs. Bassett her mother was failin' fast, and she'd better come to-day. He knew no more, and having delivered his errand he rode away, saying it looked like snow and he must be jogging, or he wouldn't get home till night.

"We must go right off, Eldad. Hitch up, and I'll be ready in less'n no time," said Mrs. Bassett, wasting not a minute in tears and lamentations, but pulling off her apron as she went in, with her head in a sad jumble of bread, anxiety, turkey, sorrow, haste, and cider apple-sauce.

A few words told the story, and the children left their work to help her get ready, mingling their grief for "Gran'ma" with regrets for the lost dinner.

"I'm dreadful sorry, dears, but it can't be helped. I couldn't cook nor eat no way, now, and if that blessed woman gets better sudden, as she has before, we'll have cause for thanksgivin', and I'll give you a dinner you won't forget in a hurry," said Mrs. Bassett, as she tied on her brown silk pumpkin-hood, with a sob for the good old mother who had made it for her.

Not a child complained after that, but ran about helpfully, bringing moccasins, heating the footstone, and getting ready for a long drive, because Gran'ma lived twenty miles away, and there were no railroads in those parts to whisk people to and fro like magic. By the time the old yellow sleigh was at the door, the bread was in the oven, and Mrs. Bassett was waiting, with her camlet cloak on, and the baby done up like a small bale of blankets.

"Now, Eph, you must look after the cattle like a man, and keep up the fires, for there's a storm brewin', and neither the children nor dumb critters must suffer," said Mr. Bassett, as he turned up the collar of his rough coat and put on his blue mittens, while the old mare shook her bells as if she preferred a trip to Keene to hauling wood all day.

"Tilly, put extry comfortables on the beds tonight, the wind is so searchin' up chamber. Have the baked beans and Injun-puddin' for dinner, and whatever you do, don't let the boys git at the mince-pies, or you'll have them down sick. I shall come back the minute I can leave Mother. Pa will come tomorrer, anyway, so keep snug and be good. I depend on you, my darter; use your jedgment, and don't let nothin' happen while Mother's away."

"Yes'm, yes'm—good-bye, good-bye!" called the children, as Mrs. Bassett was packed into the sleigh and driven away, leaving a stream of directions behind her.

Eph, the sixteen-year-old boy, immediately put on his biggest boots, assumed a sober, responsible manner, and surveyed his little responsibilities with a paternal air, drolly like his father's. Tilly tied on her mother's bunch of keys, rolled up the sleeves of her homespun gown, and began to order about the younger girls. They soon forgot poor Granny, and found it great fun to keep house all alone, for Mother seldom left home, but ruled her family in the good old-fashioned way. There were no servants, for the little daughters were Mrs. Bassett's only maids, and the stout boys helped their father, all working happily together with no wages but love; learning in the best manner the use of the heads and hands with which they were to make their own way in the world.

The few flakes that caused the farmer to predict bad weather soon increased to a regular snow-storm, with gusts of wind, for up among the hills winter came early and lingered long. But the children were busy, gay, and warm indoors, and never minded the rising gale nor the whirling white storm outside.

"Don't it look beautiful?" said Prue, when they paused to admire the general effect.

"Pretty nice, I think. I wish Ma could see how well we can do it," began Tilly, when a loud howling startled both girls, and sent them flying to the window. The short afternoon had passed so quickly that twilight had come before they knew it, and now, as they looked out through the gathering dusk, they saw four small black figures tearing up the road, to come bursting in, all screaming at once: "The bear, the bear! Eph, get the gun! He's coming, he's coming!"....

A very singular thing happened next, and all who saw it stood amazed, for suddenly Tilly threw down the ax, flung open the door, and ran straight into the arms of the bear, who stood erect to receive her, while his growlings changed to a loud "Haw, haw!" that startled the children....

"It's Gad Hopkins, tryin' to fool us!" cried Eph....

"Oh Gad, how could you scare us so?" laughed Tilly still held fast in one shaggy arm of the bear, while the other drew a dozen oranges from some deep pocket in the buffalo-skin coat....

"Come in and set up to dinner with us. Prue and I have done it all ourselves, and Pa will be along soon I reckon," cried Tilly....

"Couldn't, no ways. My folks will think I'm dead ef I don't get along home, sence

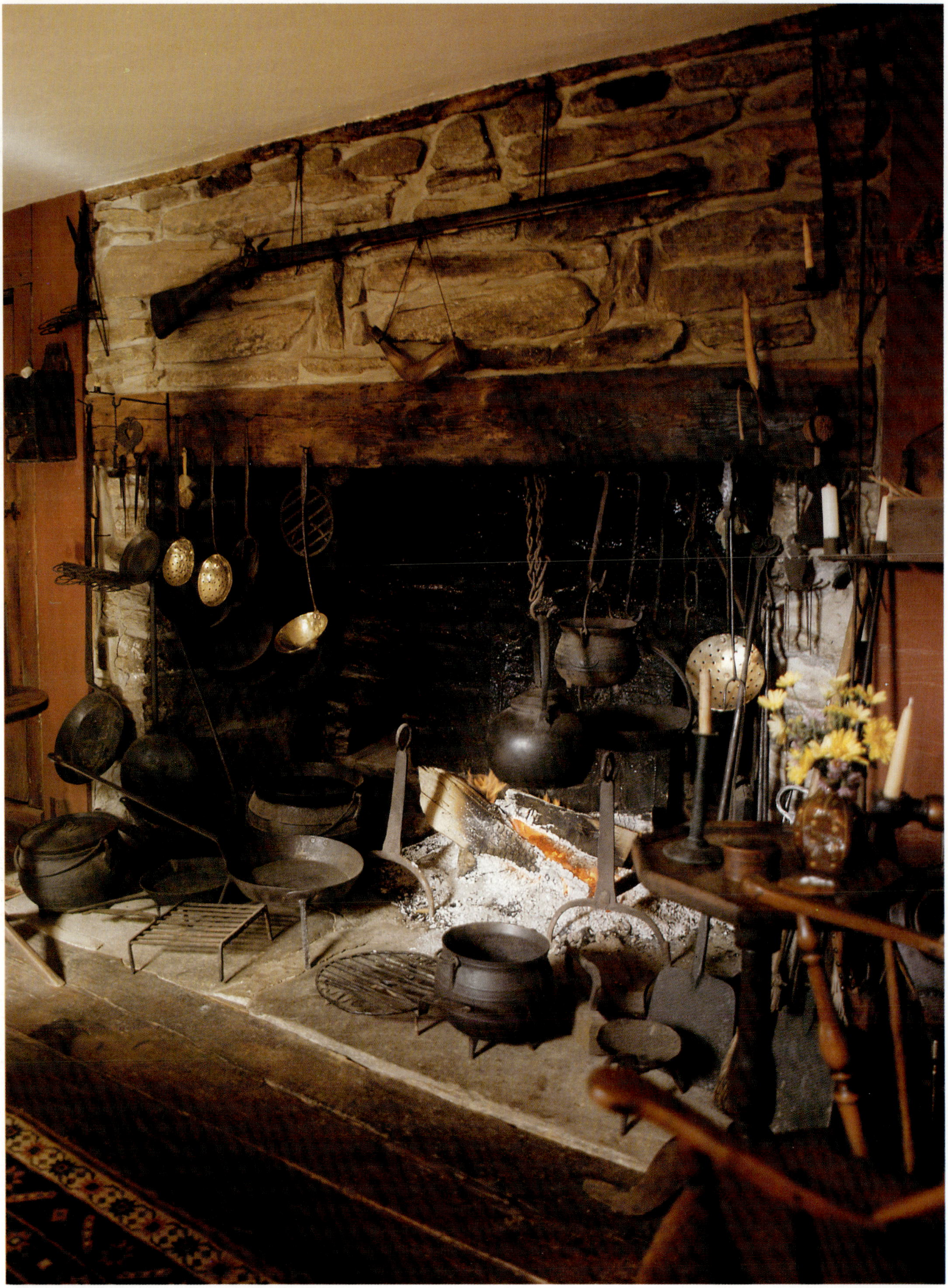

the horse and sleigh have gone ahead empty....

"My sakes alive—the turkey is burnt on one side, and the kettles have biled over so the pies I put to warm are all ashes!" scolded Tilly, as the flurry subsided and she remembered her dinner.

"Well, I can't help it. I couldn't think of victuals when I expected to be eaten alive myself, could I?" pleaded poor Prue....

Tilly laughed, and all the rest joined in, so good humor was restored, and the spirits of the younger ones were revived by sucks from the one orange which passed from hand to hand with great rapidity while the older girls dished up the dinner. They were just struggling to get the pudding out of the cloth when Roxy called out, "Here's Pa!"

"There's folks with him," added Rhody.

"Lots of 'em! I see two big sleighs chock full," shouted Seth, peering through the dusk.

"It looks like a semintary. Guess Gramma's dead and come up to be buried here," said Sol, in a solemn tone. This startling suggestion made Tilly, Prue, and Eph hasten to look out, full of dismay at such an ending of their festival.

"If that is a funeral, the mourners are uncommon jolly," said Eph, drily, as merry voices and loud laughter broke the white silence without.

"I see Aunt Cinthy, and Cousin Hetty—and there's Mose and Amos. I do declare, Pa's bringin' 'em all home to have some fun here," cried Prue, as she recognized one familiar face after another.

"Oh, my patience! Ain't I glad I got dinner, and don't I hope it will turn out good!" exclaimed Tilly, while the twins pranced with delight, and the small boys roared:

"Horray for Pa! Horray for Thanksgivin'!"

The cheer was answered heartily, and in came Father, Mother, Baby, aunts and cousins, all in great spirits, and all much surprised to find such a festive welcome awaiting them.

"Ain't Gran'ma dead at all?" asked Sol, in the midst of the kissing and handshaking.

"Bless your heart, no! It was all a mistake of old Mr. Chadwick's. He's as deaf

129

as an adder, and when Mrs. Brooks told him Mother was mendin' fast, and she wanted me to come down today, certain sure, he got the message all wrong, and give it to the fust person passin' in such a way as to scare me 'most to death, and send us down in a hurry. Mother was sittin' up as chirk as you please, and dreadful sorry you didn't all come.''

"So to keep the house quiet for her, and give you a taste of the fun, your Pa fetched us all up to spend the evenin', and we are goin' to have a jolly time on't, to dedge by the looks of things,'' said Aunt Cinthy, briskly finishing the tale when Mrs. Bassett paused for want of breath.

"What in the world put it into your head we was comin', and set you to gettin' up such a supper?'' asked Mr. Bassett, looking about him, well pleased and much surprised at the plentiful table.

Tilly modestly began to tell, but the others broke in and sang her praises in a sort of chorus, in which bears, pigs, pies, and oranges were oddly mixed. Great satisfaction was expressed by all, and Tilly and Prue were so elated by the commendation of Ma and the aunts, that they set forth their dinner, sure everything was perfect.

But when the eating began which it did the moment wraps were off, then their pride got a fall; for the first person who tasted the stuffing (it was big Cousin Mose, and that made it harder to bear) nearly choked over the bitter morsel.

"Tilly Bassett, whatever made you put wormwood and catnip in your stuffin'?'' demanded Ma, trying not to be severe, for all the rest were laughing, and Tilly looked ready to cry.

"I did it,'' said Prue, nobly taking all the blame which caused Pa to kiss her on the spot, and declare that it didn't do a mite of harm, for the turkey was all right.

"I never see onions cooked better. All the vegetables is well done, and the dinner a credit to you, my dears,'' declared Aunt Cinthy, with her mouth full of the fragrant vegetable she praised.

The pudding was an utter failure, in spite of the blazing brandy in which it lay—as hard and heavy as one of the stone balls on Squire Dunkin's great gate. It was speedily whisked out of sight, and all fell upon the pies, which were perfect. But Tilly and Prue were much depressed, and didn't recover their spirits till the dinner was over and the evening fun well underway.

"Blind-man's buff,'' "Hunt the slipper,'' "Come, Philander,'' and other lively games soon set every one bubbling over with jollity, and when Eph struck up "Money Musk'' on his fiddle, old and young fell into their places for a dance. All down the long kitchen they stood, Mr. and Mrs. Bassett at the top, the twins at the bottom, and then away they went, heeling and toeing, cutting pigeon-wings, and taking their steps in a way that would convulse modern children with their new-fangled romps called dancing. Mose and Tilly covered themselves with glory by the vigor with which they kept it up, till fat Aunt Cinthy fell into a chair, breathlessly declaring that a very little of such exercise was enough for a woman of her "heft.''

Apples and cider, chat and singing, finished the evening, and after a grand kissing all round, the guests drove away in the clear moonlight which came just in time to cheer their long drive.

When the jingle of the last bell had died away, Mr. Bassett said soberly, as they stood together on the hearth: "Children, we have special cause to be thankful that the sorrow we expected was changed into joy, so we'll read a chapter 'fore we go to bed, and give thanks where thanks is due.''

Then Tilly set out the light-stand with the big Bible on it, and a candle on each side, and all sat quietly in the fire-light, smiling as they listened with happy hearts to the sweet old words that fit all times and seasons so beautifully.

When the good-nights were over, and the children in bed, Prue put her arm around Tilly and whispered tenderly, for she felt her shake, and was sure she was crying:

"Don't mind about the old stuffin' and puddin', deary—nobody cared, and Ma said we really did do surprisin' well for such young girls.''

The laughter Tilly was trying to smother broke out then, and was so infectious, Prue could not help joining her, even before she knew the cause of the merriment.

"I was mad about the mistakes, but don't care enough to cry. I'm laughing to think how Gad fooled Eph and I found him out. I thought Mose and Amos would have died over it when I told them, it was so funny,'' explained Tilly, when she got her breath.

"I was so scared....It was real mean to frighten the little ones so,'' laughed Prue, as Tilly gave a growl.

Here a smart rap on the wall of the next room caused a sudden lull in the fun, and Mrs. Bassett's voice was heard, saying warningly, "Girls, go to sleep immediate, or you'll wake the baby.''

"Yes'm,'' answered two meek voices, and after a few irrepressible giggles, silence reigned, broken only by an occasional snore from the boys, or the soft scurry of mice in the buttery, taking their part in this old-fashioned Thanksgiving.

A Thanksgiving Anthology

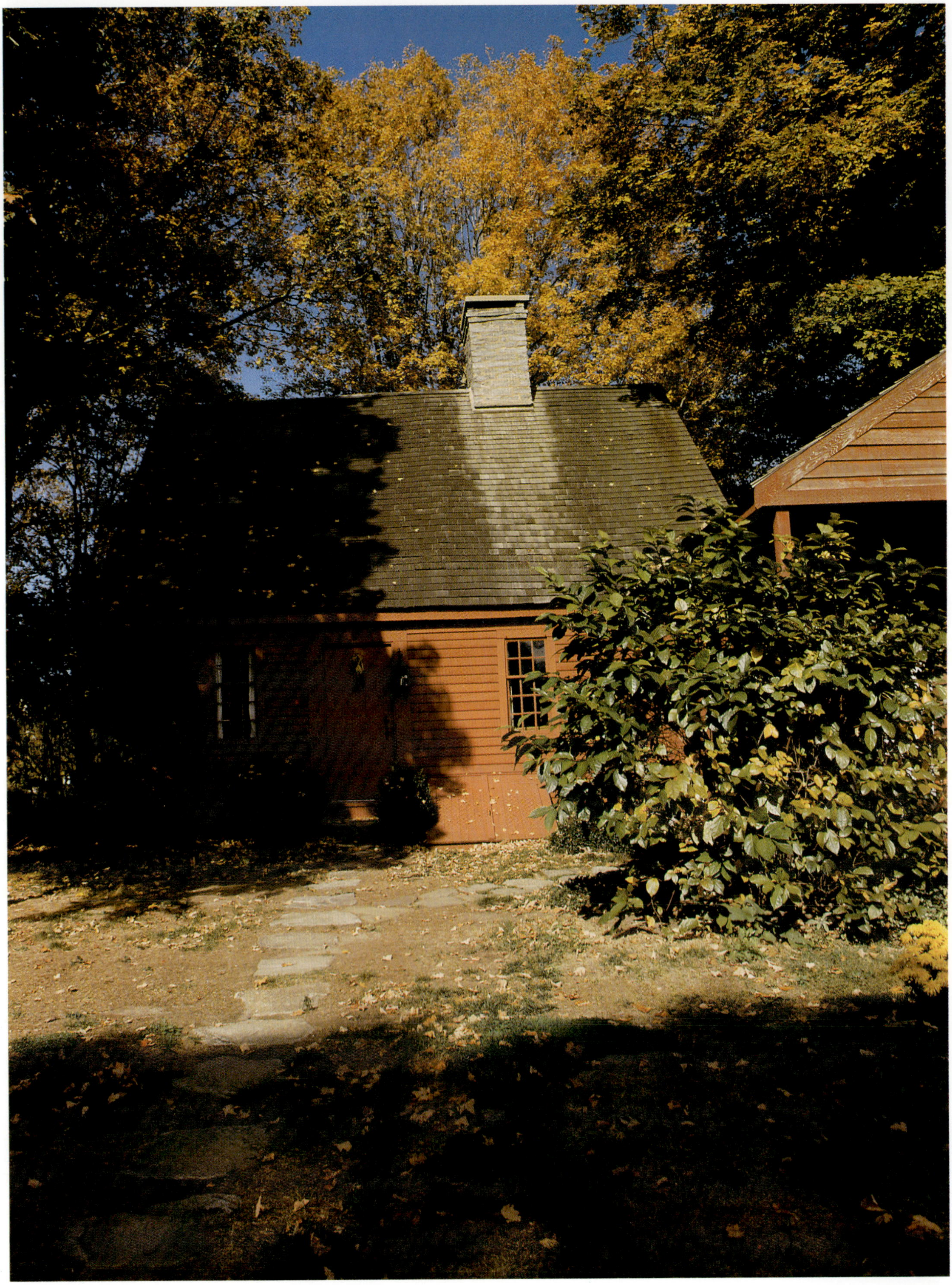

When they woke, like early birds, [the next day] it still snowed, but up the little Bassetts jumped, broke the ice in their pitchers, and went down with cheeks glowing like winter apples, after a brisk scrub and scramble into their clothes. Eph was off to the barn, and Tilly soon had a great kettle of mush ready, which, with milk warm from the cows, made a wholesome breakfast for the seven hearty children.

"Now about dinner," said the young housekeeper, as the pewter spoons stopped clattering, and the earthen bowls stood empty.

"Ma said, have what we liked, but she didn't expect us to have a real Thanksgiving dinner, because she won't be here to cook it, and we don't know how," began Prue, doubtfully.

"I can roast a turkey and make a pudding as well as anybody, I guess. The pies are all ready, and if we can't boil vegetables and so on, we don't deserve any dinner," cried Tilly, burning to distinguish herself, and bound to enjoy the utmost her brief authority.

"Yes, yes!" cried all the boys, "let's have a dinner anyway; Ma won't care, and the good victuals will spoil if they ain't eaten right up."

"Pa is coming tonight, so we won't have dinner till late; that will be real genteel and give us plenty of time," added Tilly, suddenly realizing the novelty of the task she had undertaken.

"Did you ever roast a turkey?" asked Roxy, with an air of deep interest.

"Should you darst to try?" said Rhody, in an awe-stricken tone.

"You will see what I can do. Ma said I was to use my jedgment about things, and I'm going to. All you children have got to do is keep out of the way, and let Prue and me work. Eph, I wish you'd put a fire in the best room, so the little ones can play in there. We shall want the settin'-room for the table, and I won't have 'em pickin' 'round when we get things fixed," commanded Tilly, bound to make her short reign a brilliant one.

"I don't know about that. Ma didn't tell us to," began cautious Eph, who felt that this invasion of the sacred best parlor was a daring step.

"Don't we always do it Sundays and Thanksgivings? Wouldn't Ma wish the children kept safe and warm anyhow? Can I get up a nice dinner with four rascals under my feet all the time? Come, now, if you want roast turkey and onions, plum-puddin' and mince-pie, you'll have to do as I tell you, and be lively about it."

Tilly spoke with such spirit, and her last suggestion was so irresistible, that Eph gave in, and, laughing good-naturedly, tramped away to heat up the best room, devoutly hoping that nothing serious would happen to punish such audacity.

The young folks delightedly trooped in to destroy the order of that prim apartment with housekeeping under the black horse-hair sofa, "horseback riders" on the arms of the best rocking-chair, and an Indian war-dance all over the well-waxed furniture. Eph, finding the society of the peaceful sheep and cows more to his mind than that of two excited sisters, lingered over his chores in the barn as long as possible, and left the girls in peace.

Now Tilly and Prue were in their glory, and as soon as the breakfast things were out of the way, they prepared for a grand cooking-time. They were handy girls, though they had never heard of a cooking-school, never touched a piano, and knew nothing of embroidery beyond the samples which hung framed in the parlor; one ornamented with a pink mourner under a blue weeping-willow, the other with this pleasing verse each word being done in a different color, which gave the effect of a distracted rainbow:

"This sampler neat was worked by me,

In my twelfth year, Prudence B."

Both rolled up their sleeves, put on their largest aprons, and got out all the spoons, dishes, pots, and pans they could find, "so as to have everything handy," as Prue said.

"Now, sister, we'll have dinner at five; Pa will be here by that time if he is coming tonight, and be so surprised to find us all ready, for he won't have any very nice victuals if Gran'ma is so sick," said Tilly importantly. "I shall give the children a piece at noon" (Tilly meant luncheon); "doughnuts and cheese, with apple-pie and cider will please 'em. There's beans for Eph; he likes cold pork, so we won't stop to warm it up, for there's lots to do, and I don't mind saying to you I'm dreadful dubersome about the turkey."

"It's all ready but the stuffing, and roasting is as easy as can be. I can baste first rate. Ma always likes to have me, I'm so patient and stiddy, she says," answered Prue, for the responsibility of this great undertaking did not rest upon her, so she took a cheerful view of things.

"I know, but it's the stuffin' that troubles me," said Tilly, rubbing her round elbows as she eyed the immense fowl laid out on a platter before her. "I don't know how much I want, nor what sort of yarbs to put in, and he's so awful big, I'm kind of afraid of him."

"I ain't! I fed him all summer, and he never gobbled at *me*. I feel real mean to be thinking of gobbling him, poor old chap," laughed Prue, patting her departed pet with an air of mingled affection and appetite.

"Well, I'll get the puddin' off my mind fust, for it ought to bile all day. Put the big kettle on, and see that the spit is clean, while I get ready."

Prue obediently tugged away at the crane, with its black hooks, from which hung the iron tea-kettle and three-legged pot; then she settled the long spit in the grooves made for it in the tall andirons, and put the dripping-pan underneath, for in those days meat was roasted as it should be, not baked in ovens.

Meantime Tilly attacked the plum-pudding. She felt pretty sure of coming out right, here, for she had seen her mother do it so many times, it looked very easy. So in went suet and fruit; all sorts of spice, to be sure she got the right ones, and brandy instead of wine. But she forgot both sugar and salt, and tied it in the cloth so tightly that it had no room to swell, so it would come out as heavy as lead and as hard as a cannon-ball, if the bag did not burst and spoil it all. Happily unconscious of these mistakes, Tilly popped it into the pot, and proudly watched it bobbing about before she put the cover on and left it to its fate.

"I can't remember what flavorin' Ma puts in," she said, when she had got her bread well soaked for the stuffing. "Sage and onions and apple-sauce go with goose, but I can't feel sure of anything but pepper and salt for a turkey."

"Ma puts in some kind of mint, I know,

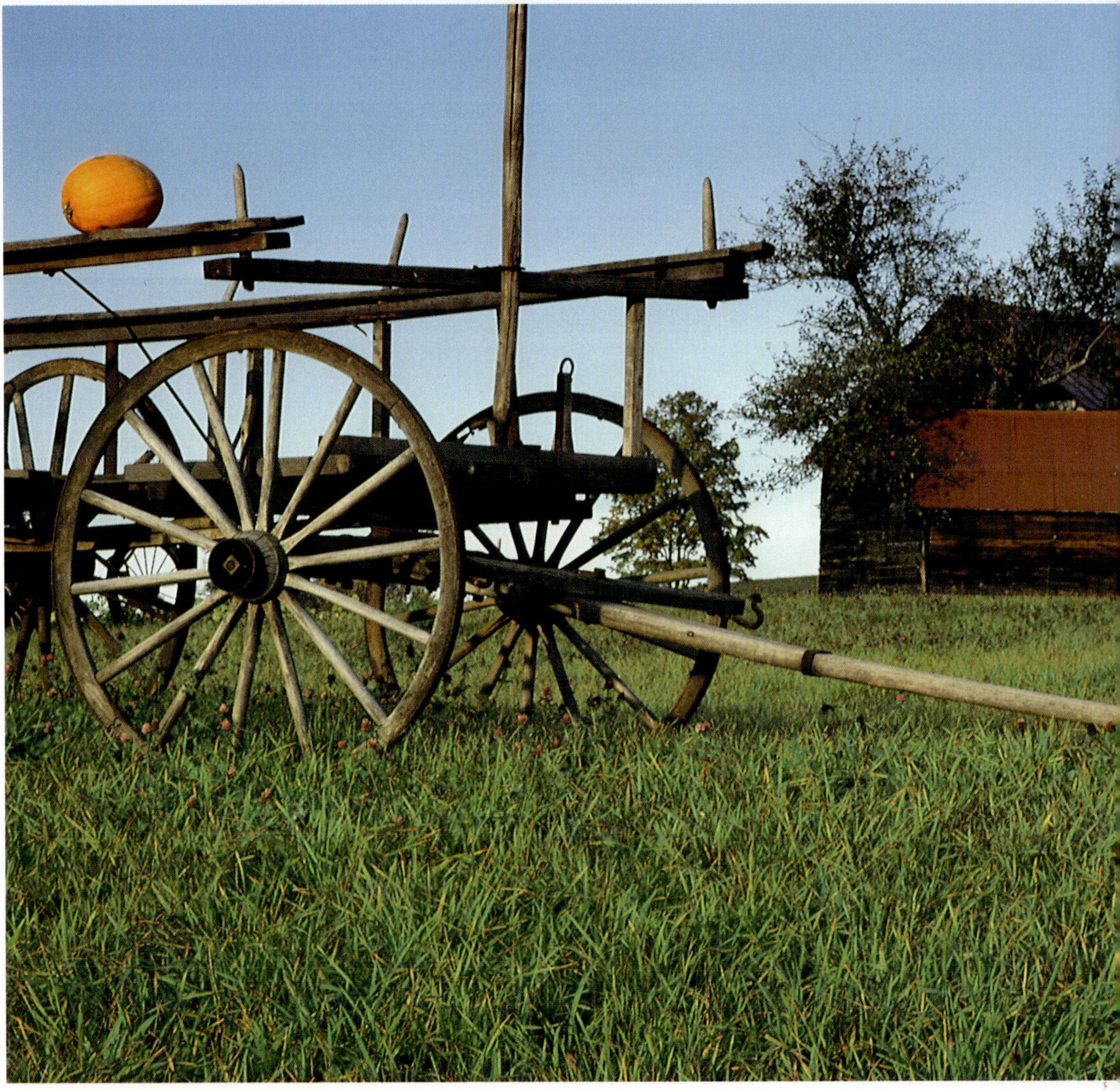

but I forget whether it is spearmint, peppermint, or pennyroyal," answered Prue, in a tone of doubt, but trying to show her knowledge of "yarbs," or, at least, of their names.

"Seems to me it's sweet marjoram or summer savory. I guess we'll put both in, and then we are sure to be right. The best is up garret; you run and get some, while I mash the bread," commanded Tilly, diving into the mess.

Away trotted Prue, but in her haste she got catnip and wormwood, for the garret was darkish, and Prue's little nose was so full of the smell of the onions she had been peeling, that everything smelt of them. Eager to be of use, she pounded up the herbs and scattered the mixture with a liberal hand into the bowl.

"It doesn't smell just right, but I suppose it will when it is cooked," said Tilly, and she filled the empty stomach, that seemed aching for food, and sewed it up with the blue yarn, which happened to be handy. She forgot to tie down his legs and wings, but she set him by till his hour came, well satisfied with her work.

"Shall we roast the little pig, too? I think he'd look nice with a necklace of sausages, as Ma fixed one last Christmas," asked Prue, elated with their success.

"I couldn't do it. I loved that little pig, and cried when he was killed. I should feel as if I was roasting the baby," answered Tilly, glancing toward the buttery where piggy hung, looking so pink and pretty it certainly did seem cruel to eat him.

It took a long time to get all the vegetables ready, for, as the cellar was full, the girls thought they would have every sort. Eph helped, and by noon all was ready for cooking, and the cranberry-sauce, a good deal scorched, was cooling in the lean-to.

Luncheon was a lively meal, and doughnuts and cheese vanished in such quantities that Tilly feared no one would have an appetite for her sumptuous dinner. The boys assured her they would be starving by five o'clock, and Sol mourned bitterly over the little pig that was not to be served up.

"Now you all go and coast, while Prue and I set the table and get out the best chiny," said Tilly, bent on having her dinner look well, no matter what its other failings might be.

Out came the rough sleds, on went the round hoods, old hats, red cloaks, and moccasins, and away trudged the four younger Bassets, to disport themselves in the snow, and try the ice down by the old mill, where the great wheel turned and so splashed so merrily in the summer-time.

Eph took his fiddle and scraped away to his heart's content in the parlor, while the girls, after a short rest, set the table and made all ready to dish up the dinner when that exciting moment came. It was not at all the sort of table we see now, but would look very plain and countrified to us, with its green-handled knives and two-pronged steel forks; its red-and-white china, and pewter platters, scoured till they shone, with mugs and spoons to match, and a brown jug for the cider. The cloth was coarse, but white as snow, and the little maids had seen the blue-eyed flax grow, out of which their mother wove the linen they had watched and watered while it bleached in the green meadow. They had no napkins and little silver; but the best tankard and Ma's few wedding spoons were set forth in state. Nuts and apples at the corners gave an air, and the place of honor was left in the middle for the oranges yet to come.

Thanksgiving Time

When all the leaves are off the boughs,
And nuts and apples gathered in,
And cornstalks waiting for the sows,
And pumpkins safe in barn and bin,
Then Mother says, "My children dear,
The fields are brown, and autumn flies;
Thanksgiving Day is very near,
And we must make thanksgiving pies!"

—ANONYMOUS

FROM *Thanksgiving: A Poem in Two Parts*

The Cookery now goes on, the baking's laid,
And many a mammoth pie and pudding's
  made,
Roast meat and gingerbread and custards
  rare,
Are seen and smelt and tasted everywhere,
Plum-cakes and sweet-meats of all kinds
  abound,
And pumpkin pies ranged in platoons are
  found;
The country floats with dainties fit for kings,
And inundation of the choicest things.

—HENRY BLISS

The Feast-Time of the Year

This is the feast-time of the year,
When plenty pours her wine of cheer,
And even humble boards may spare
To poorer poor a kindly share.
While bursting barns and granaries know
A richer, fuller overflow.
And they who dwell in golden ease
Blest without toil, yet toil to please.

—ANONYMOUS

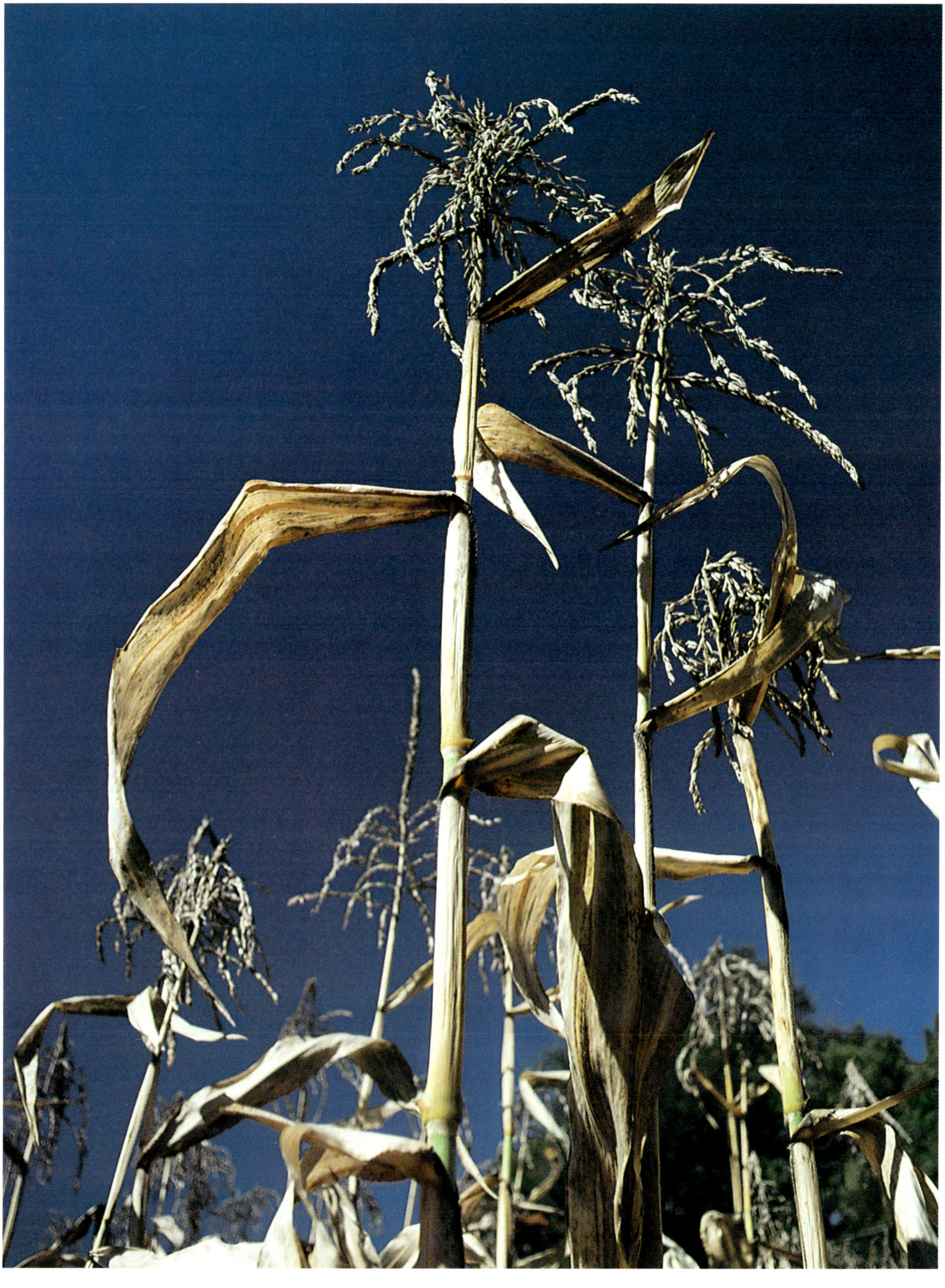

Cousin Nanette's Story

"Auntie, tell us all a story! do!"

"No! you must tell me one. I want to hear
About your pleasant life."
"I have no skill
At story-telling craft, but sister Nan
Is always ready with some lively talk;
Let's call on her."
Nannette shook back her hair,
"I'll tell you, if you'll listen long and well,
A true Thanksgiving story."
So she told,

ONE THANKSGIVING

OUT in the beautiful country,
    When the yellow moon was high,
When the Autumn fruits were garnered,
    And the Winter nights were nigh,

Old Farmer Pratt was counting
    His herds of lowing kine,
His sheep with growing fleeces,
    His lazy, fattened swine;

And, as he reckoned slowly,
    The calm and frosty night
Called him to barn and sheepfold,
    To see if all was right.

Under a sheltering hay-rick
    He paused to muse awhile,
When two young voices near him
    Awoke a passing smile:

One was his eldest daughter,
    Priscilla speaking low,
And the other was one of the neighbors,
    He guessed, but he did not know.

"I can't!" Priscilla was saying,
    "I can't! it's going too far;
It would make me doubly wretched
    To be deceiving ma.

And father"—he felt the shudder
    That he could not hear or see;
And he said, "I b'lieve Priscilla
    Is fairly afraid of me.

She's a skeery thing, like her mother;
    But I vow I didn't suppose
The words I've said so keerless
    Was goin' home so close.

I've laughed about Reuben, and called him
    A sort of a shiftless lad,
But I never supposed the fellow
    Was anything very bad.

It seems he's been coaxin' and teasin'
    My Prissie to run away;
It can't do no harm, (I'm her father,)
    To listen to what they say.

If he gives her up for fear o' me,
    I don't think much o' him,
And I wonder, should she lose him,
    Would it make her bright eyes dim?''

"Priscilla, darling,'' 'twas Reuben,
    Speaking soft and low-
"I've waited in hope and patience
    Two weary years, you know,

And loved you as only a man loves
    The woman he means to wed;
And only for your sake, Prissie,
    No words have I ever said

To any one on the subject;
    But to-night—now, listen, dear!
We must have this matter settled;
    I can't wait another year.

I'll talk with your father to-morrow,
    And learn his objections to me.''
"Oh, no!" said Priscilla in terror,
    For then he would think that we—

That I—had been talking about him,
    And that makes him angriest of all.''
Then Reuben's voice grew firmer,
    And seemed to clearer fall:

"Your father is not an ogre;
    I do not dread his wrath,
'Tis better for us to be honest,
    And keep a straightforward path.

But I know what a faint-hearted chicken
    You are, and have always been,
And though I believe your father
    Is one of the best of men.

If he hates me as bad as you think for,
    Of course, he'll refuse outright,
All consent to our future wedding,
    And leaves us no chance for flight;

For you never would dare to marry
    Right in the face and eyes
Of his plain commands against it,
    Though they be neither kind nor wise.

I've nothing to say of your parents,
    They're honest, and true, and good,
You've served them and loved and obeyed them,
    As a dutiful daughter should.

But I've made up my mind to one thing:
    If you persistently say
That I mustn't speak to your father,
    Why, then, we must run away.''

"Oh, Reuben!'' "Now Prissie, darling,
    I leave it to you to choose,
I've lost my heart and my patience,
    But my wife I'm not willing to lose.

I shan't discuss the subject
    By another word to-night,
But the day before Thanksgiving,
    If everything's fair and bright,

I'll hitch up my roan colt Major,
    And drive to the village, and see
If old Parson Emerson's willing
    To do a favor for me.

And then, when the stars are shining—''
    The young folks moved away,
And old Farmer Pratt stared, dumbly,
    With his head against the hay.

Next morning he watched Priscilla,
    Her blue eyes were swimming in tears,
And her quivering chin told plainly
    That her heart was full of fears.

Sometimes she'd look so earnest,
    As though she had something to say;
Then the tears would seem to choke her,
    And she'd turn her head away.

But the day before Thanksgiving
    Dawned crisp and bright and clear,
And every farmer's kitchen
    Was crowded with good cheer.

All day the wide brick ovens
    Were kept at pie-bake heat,
And merry voices echoed
    To the tread of busy feet.

All day the golden cider
    Slow trickled from the mill,
And all day long the farmer
    Was thinking, thinking still;

Towards night he jammed his hat on
    With most unusual vim,
And went across the meadow
    At a rapid stride, for him.

And then, ten minutes later,
    He paused beside a door
That he left in bitter anger
    Some fifteen years before.

Out stepped a cheery matron:
    "Why, Brother Pratt! You here?
I'm sure I'm glad to see you;
    Walk in and take a cheer.

The weather's getting chilly.
    How is your wife this fall?
I often see your boys round,
    Handsome, and strong, and tall.''

And so she chatted lightly,
    With deft, unconscious air,
And never even hinted
    'Twas strange to see him there.

But while he questioned to himself
    If she'd take Reuben's part,
The outer door swung slowly,
    And in walked Deacon Hart;

No angry words were spoken,
    But Farmer Pratt learned then
That the plan he had discovered
    Was all unknown to them;

The young folks asked no favors;
    They knew an old feud lay
Smouldering between the fathers;
    So they would run away.

But when the two men parted
    Beside the meadow stile,
Both faces wrinkled kindly
    With a grim and sober smile.

Hours after came the roan colt,
    Shaking his handsome head,
The bells were off the harness,
    And he seemed to lightly tread.

Priscilla hushed her sobbing.
    And hurried down the stair;
But just as she was stepping
    Out into the frosty air,

The kitchen-door flew open,
    Two tallow-dips ablaze
Filled her with sudden terror,
    And Reuben with amaze;

But her father's voice was calling:
    "Here, John, you hurry now—
Go get the ewe and cossets;
    Drive round the brindle cow;

Roll out that barrel of apples,
    And the white Chenangoes fine;
And bring a keg of cider,
    And a jug of currant wine.

Willie, tie up the feather bed,
    And put the pillows in;
And, mother, where's the pillow-slips,
    And sheets and quilts and things?

Bring out the new rose blankets
    That in the clothes-press lay;
Prissie must have her setting out—
    She's going to run away.''

Imagine all the wonder
    That from this was sure to come!
Imagine tears and kisses
    Thrown in *ad libitum!*

And two shame faced young people
    Waiting another day,
And then concluding quietly
    They wouldn't run away.

The happiest Thanksgiving
    That e'er New England knew
Dawned on the village homes next day,
    Where hearts beat warm and true.

Old feuds were all forgotten—
    Old troubles lain aside—
And Reuben lived to bless the day
    He won his happy bride.

—NANETTE SNOW EMERSON

The Doxology

Thomas Ken, 1692

Louis Bourgeois, 1551

Praise God from whom all blessings flow; Praise Him, all creatures here below; Praise Him above, ye heav'nly host: Praise Father, Son, and Holy Ghost. A-men.

A Thanksgiving Anthology

Down In My Heart

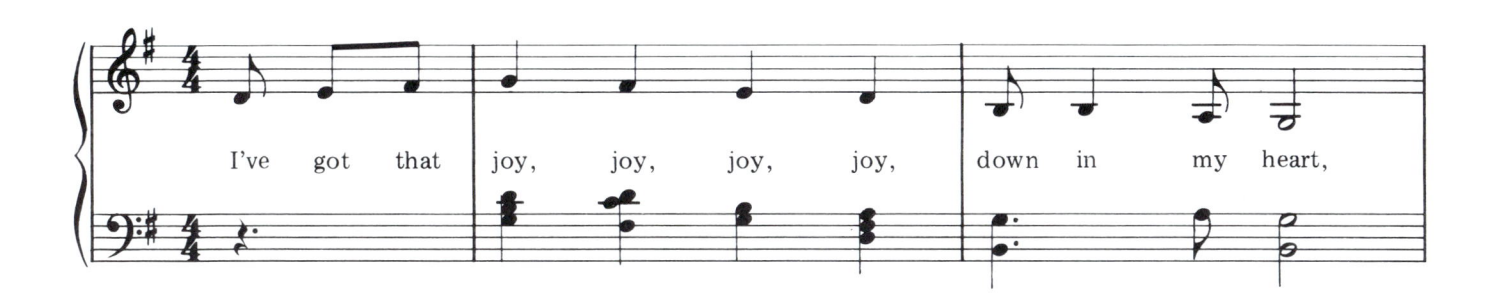

I've got that joy, joy, joy, joy, down in my heart, down in my heart, down in my heart. I've got that joy, joy, joy, joy, down in my heart, down in my heart to-day.

Prayer Before Eating

Our father, hear us, and our grandfather. I mention also all those that shine, the yellow day, the good wind, the good timber, and the good earth.

All the animals, listen to me under the ground. Animals above ground, and water animals, listen to me. We shall eat your remnants of food. Let them be good.

Let there be long breath and life. Let the people increase, the children of all ages, the girls and the boys, and the men of all ages and the women, the old men of all ages and the old women. The food will give us strength whenever the sun runs.

Listen to us, Father, Grandfather. We ask thought, heart, love, happiness. We are going to eat.

—ARAPAHO

The Hebrew Morning Service

Though our mouths were full of song as the sea,
and our tongues of exultation as the multitude of its waves,
and our lips of praise as the wide-extended firmament;
though our eyes shone with light like the sun and the moon,
and our hands were spread forth like the eagles of heaven,
and our feet were swift as hinds,
we should still be unable to thank thee and bless thy name,
O Lord our God and God of our fathers,
for one thousandth or one ten thousandth part
of the bounties which thou hast bestowed upon our fathers and upon us.

—from THE HEBREW PRAYER BOOK

Thanksgiving Day

'Tis the happiest day of all the year,
    When gathered round the festal board,
Our hearts are filled with grateful cheer,
    We render thanks to our dear Lord.
Thanks for every blessing
    That he has o'er us cast;
Ever watching and carressing
    When threatened by the stormy blast.
And so we pray He'll still watch o'er
    'Til this short life is past,
And bring us to that golden shore
    Where blessings endless last.

I.

Thanksgiving Day! in youthful dreams
    Of thee, what glowing scenes arise,
Of turkey roast and cider streams,
    And monstrous pumpkin pies.

How many nights I sleepless pass'd
    In thinking of its pleasures;
And when the day did come at last,
    And grandmama produced her treasures,

Greedy of them I ate and laughed,
    And if stories may be trusted,
I always grinned, and ate, and quaffed
    Until I nearly 'busted.'

And now, I'm come to man's estate,
    To me 'tis little joy
To think, I love a heaping plate
    As much as when a boy.

And so on each Thanksgiving Day,
    I vainly look around;
I vainly look, and vainly pray,
    For the joys in youth I found.

II.

Sisters, I would woo a measure
    That should to your minds recall,
Thanksgiving Day and its merry pleasures
    That we enjoyed at "Elmwood Hall."

Was there ever a fairer scene
    Than greeted our eyes that day?
Was there ever a host of nobler mein,
    With a cheerier laugh or a merrier way?

Methinks I see him now,
    And hear his merry voice,
And I mark his open brow
    As he bids us all rejoice.

And then I think of his lady fair,
    And where will you find such another?
Who watched us with tenderest care,
    Watched, as can only a mother.

We'll think of their daughters, I ween,
    And in after years remember well,
For where is one that has seen,
    And not felt their potent spell?

Mary, quick, with pert reply,
    Saucy to the last;
Aggie, fair, with merry eye,
    And smile that holds us fast.

Let us with their guests a moment tarry,
    And think of the girls from Troy:
Of Jeannie, and Bessie and Arrie,
    And Mame, with laugh of joy.

Jennie Demarest and wise Clara Young,
    We'll still remember you,
And Jeannie, my sister, what need of this tongue
    Repeating its affection anew.

And Annie, what shall I say of you
    Before I close this rhyme?
Why, here I pledge you friendship true,
    That shall only end with time.

And I trust each one remembers
    The pleasures we enjoyed that day;
So quick, let us smother the embers,
    Lest we mourn that they've vanished away.

And I trust we may all meet again,
    Amid just as fair a scene,
And if we're old women and men,
    We'll talk of the day in memory green.

The feast is o'er, the guests are fled,
    And we are gliding down life's stream
    With shadows dark and sunlight gleam,
To mingle with the dead.
What wonder that we'll sigh at last,
    When gathered round the blazing fire,
    Grandmama old or gray-haired sire,
We think upon our pleasures past.
But soon we'll wipe our tears away,
    And as we're gathered to our rest,
    Think our lives at least were blest
With one THANKSGIVING DAY.

—DON ADOLPHUS

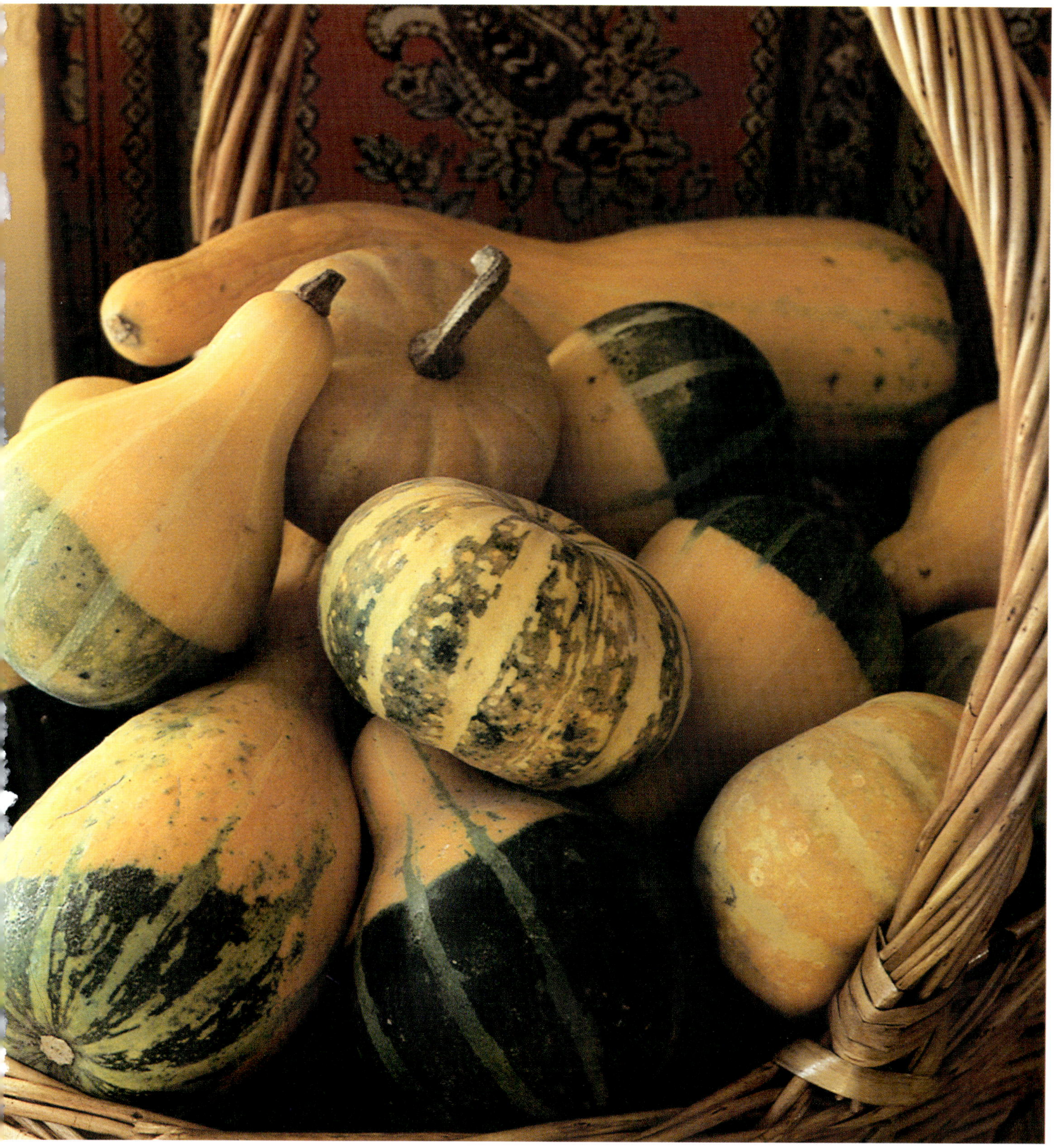

Thanks

Thank you very much indeed,
River, for your waving reed;
Hollyhocks, for budding knobs;
Foxgloves, for your velvet fobs;
Pansies, for your silly cheeks;
Chaffinches, for singing beaks;
Spring, for wood anemones
Near the mossy toes of trees;
Summer for the fruited pear,
Yellowing crab, and cherry fare;
Autumn, for the bearded load,
Hazelnuts along the road;
Winter, for the fairy-tale,
A pitting log and bouncing hail.

But, blest Father, high above,
All these joys are from Thy love;
And Your children everywhere,
Born in palace, lane, or square,
Cry with voices all agreed,
"Thank You very much indeed."

—Norman Gale

A Good Thanksgiving

Said old Gentleman Gay, "On a Thanksgiving Day,
If you want a good time, then give something away."

So he sent a fat turkey to Shoemaker Price,
And the shoemaker said, "What a big bird! How nice!
And, since a good dinner's before me, I ought
To give poor Widow Lee the small chicken I bought."

"This fine chicken, oh see!" said the pleased Widow Lee,
"And the kindness that sent it, how precious to me!
I would like to make someone as happy as I—
I'll give Washwoman Biddy my big pumpkin pie."

"And oh, sure!" Biddy said, " 'Tis the queen of all pies!
Just to look at its yellow face gladdens my eyes!
Now it's my turn, I think, and a sweet ginger cake
For the motherless Finnigan children I'll bake."

"A sweet cake, all our own! 'Tis too good to be true!"
Said the Finnigan children, Rose, Denny, and Hugh;
"It smells sweet of spice, and we'll carry a slice
To poor little lame Jake, who has nothing that's nice."

"Oh, I thank you, and thank you!" said little lame Jake,
"Oh, what a beautiful, beautiful, beautiful cake!
And oh, such a big slice! I will save all the crumbs,
And will give 'em to each little sparrow that comes!"

And the sparrows they twittered, as if they would say,
Like old Gentleman Gay, "On a Thanksgiving Day,
If you want a good time, then give something away!"

—MARIAN DOUGLAS

Turkey in the Straw

As I was a going on down the road, With a tired team and a heavy load, I cracked my whip and the leader sprung Says I good-bye to the wagon tongue. Turkey in the straw, Turkey in the hay, Roll-'em twist 'em up a high tuck-a-haw, And hit up a tune called Turkey in the straw.

2. Went out to milk and I didn't know how —
   Milked the goat instead of a cow,
   A monkey sitting on a pile of straw,
   Winking his eye at his mother-in-law.

3. Met a big catfish coming down the stream,
   Says the big catfish, "What do you mean?"
   Caught the big catfish right on the snout,
   And turned the catfish inside out.

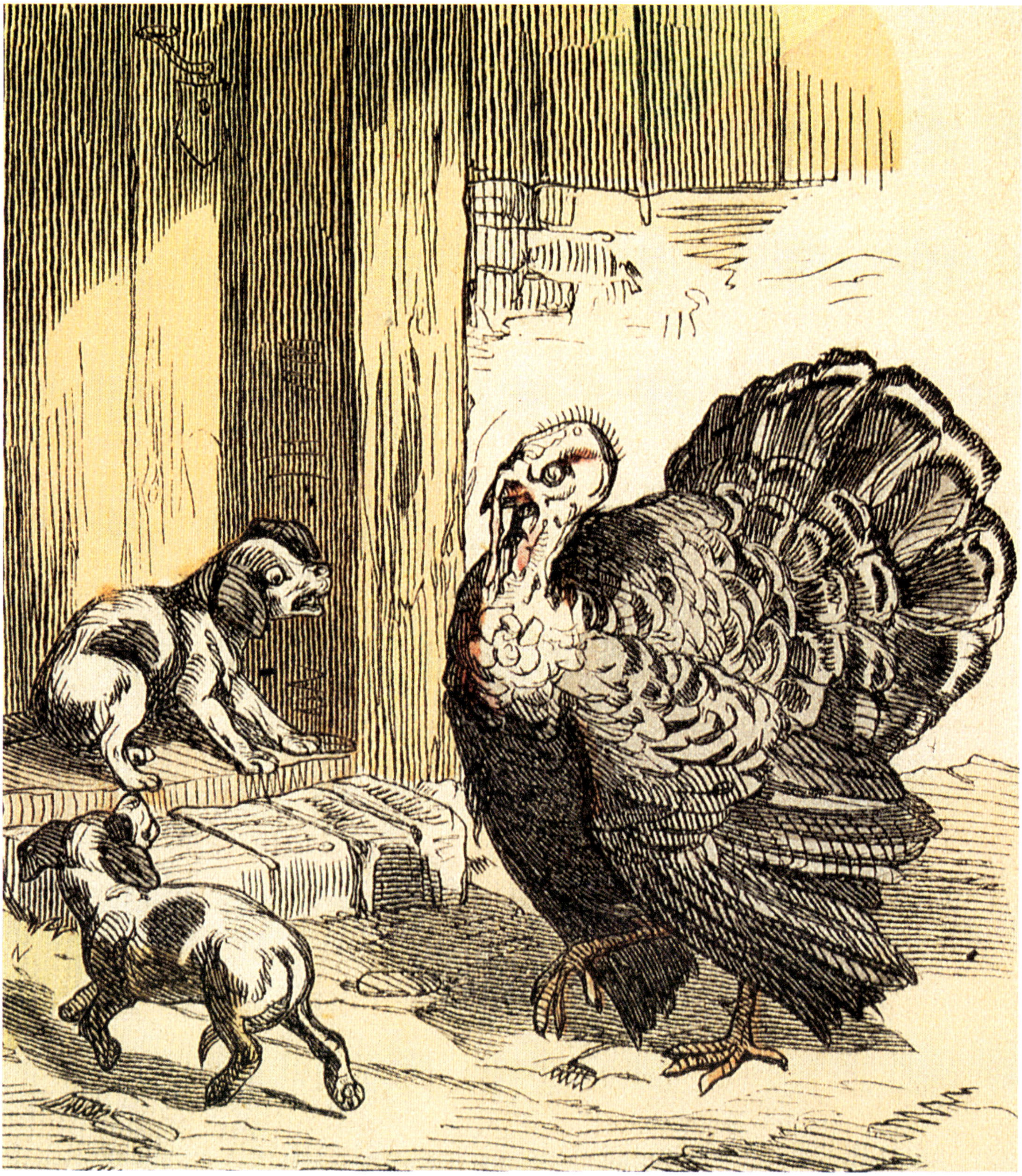

Macy's Thanksgiving Book

Simple Gifts

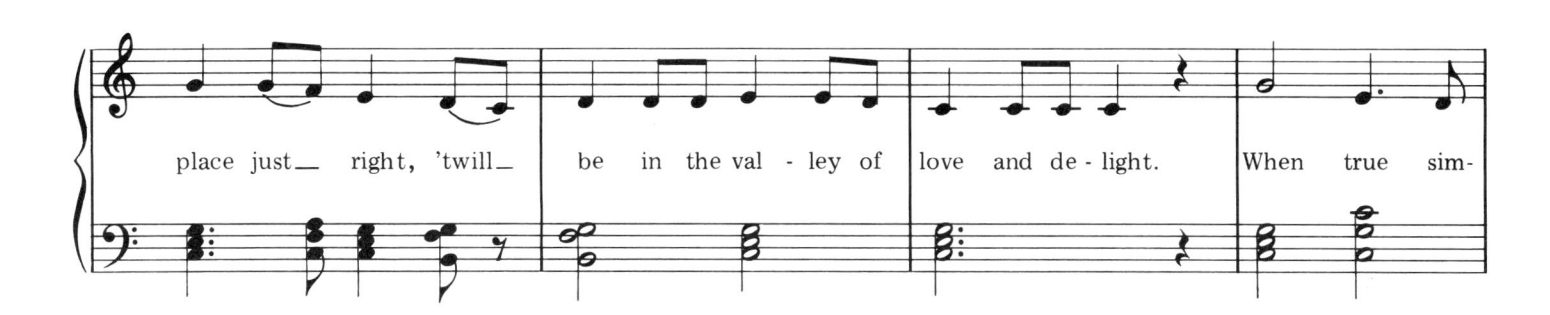

'Tis a gift to be sim-ple 'tis a gift to be free, 'tis a gift to come down where we ought to be. And when we're in the place just right, 'twill be in the val-ley of love and de-light. When true sim-pli-ci-ty is gained, to bow and to bend we will not be a-shamed. To turn, to turn 'twill be our de-light, 'til by turn-ing, turn-ing we come 'round right.

FROM *Thanksgiving Eve*

"They round the ingle form a circle wide."
—Robert Burns

    THANKSGIVING! hail thy festive cheer,
Thou day to all New-England dear!
When Labor by his mattock throws,
And gives his toil-strained nerves repose;
And Care, for want with whom to stay,
Goes off to have a holiday.
When scores of craking fowls must die,
To make the needful chicken-pie;
And turkies, twirling at the fire,
Roast, as the de'il will roast a liar;
And buxom dames, and lasses fair,
The Pilgrim's yearly feast prepare.
When Plenty gives from out her store
A dainty bit, to glad the poor,
And Want, with e'en his stingy grip,
Is lavish of his only fip.
When forge and smithy, shop and mill,
In Sabbath quietude are still,
And artisans of every grade
Are in their very best arrayed;
And cotters, in their homespun own,
Would scorn the wardrobe of a throne.
    Thanksgiving! day of all the year!
Ancient and honored custom dear!
When foes with kindlier feelings greet;
When friends, long separated, meet
To knit anew the ties that bind
Kindred to kindred, mind to mind.
When from the towers, in morning time,
Is wafted forth the tuneful chime,
When all the true its call obey,
And tune their hearts to praise and pray,
And up to Zion's courts repair
To dwell upon God's mercies there.

—Josiah Dean Canning

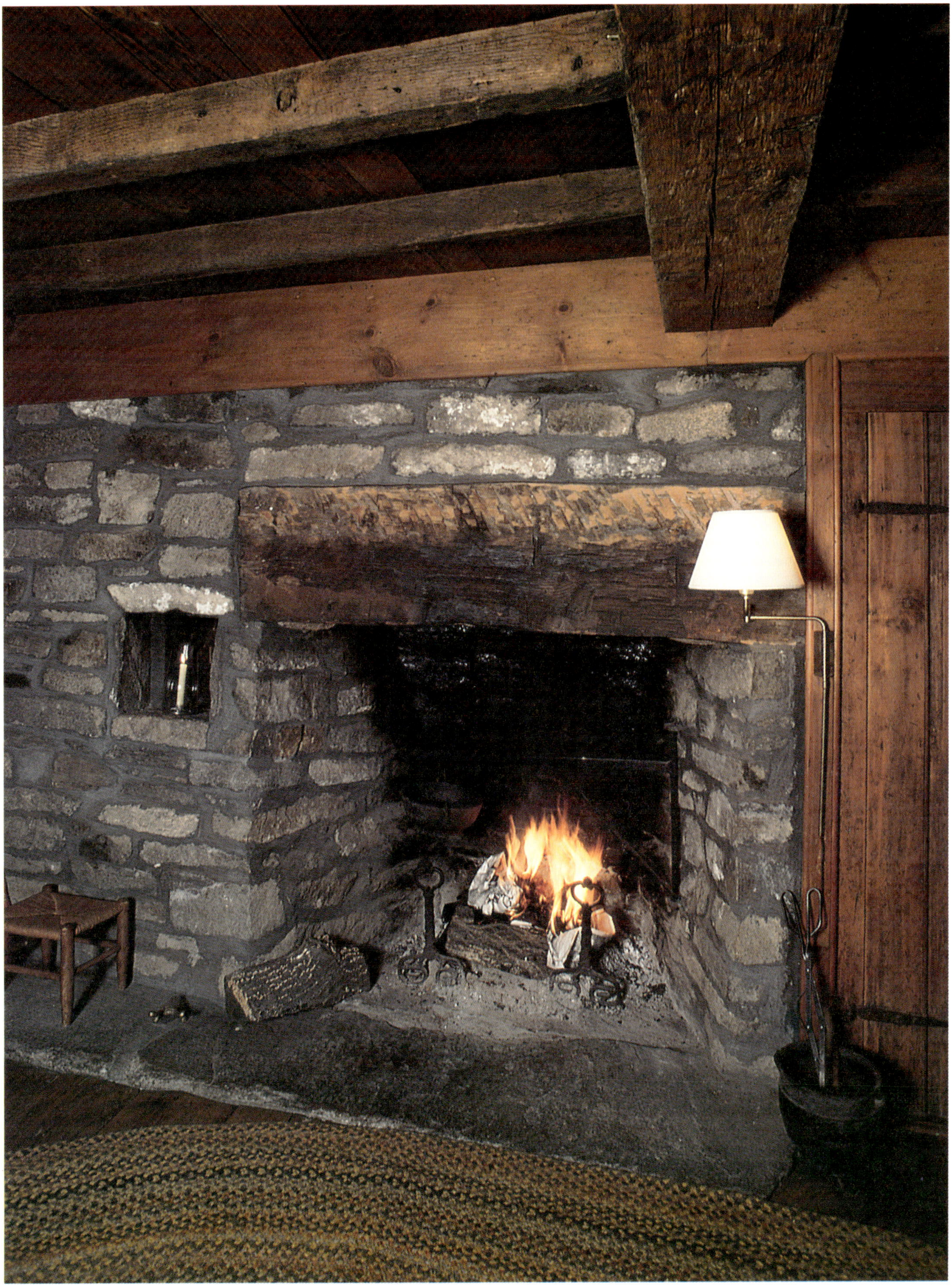

Bibliography

The following is a list of children's books for the whole family to enjoy. Some are to be read aloud; others are to be savored alone in a quiet moment. The asterisk denotes picture books for the younger children.

An Old-Fashioned Thanksgiving
Louisa May Alcott
Philadelphia: J.B. Lippincott Company, 1974

Thanksgiving
Margaret Baldwin
New York: Franklin Watts, 1983

*****Sometime's It's Turkey, Sometimes It's Feathers**
Lorna Balian
New York: Abingdon Press, 1973

First Thanksgiving
Lena Barksdale
New York: Knopf, 1942

Turkeys, Pilgrims, and Indian Corn: The Story of the Thanksgiving Symbols
Edna Barth
New York: A Clarion Book (The Seabury Press), 1975

Feast of Thanksgiving: The First American Holiday (A Play)
June Behrens
Chicago: A Golden Gate Junior Book (Childrens Press), 1974

*****Arthur's Thanksgiving**
Marc Brown
Boston: An Atlantic Monthly Press Book (Little, Brown and Co.), 1983

*****Molly's Pilgrim**
Barbara Cohen
New York: Lothrop, Lee and Shepard, 1983

The Thanksgiving Visitor
Truman Capote
New York: Random House, 1968

*****Thanksgiving Story**
Alice Dalgliesh
New York: Scribners, 1954

*****Cranberry Thanksgiving**
Wende and Harry Devlin
New York: Four Winds Press, 1971

Thanksgiving Day
Gail Gibbons
New York: A Holiday House Book, 1983

*****The Little Witch's Thanksgiving**
Linda Glovach
Englewood Cliffs, NJ: Prentice-Hall, 1976

The Harvest Feast: Stories of Yesterday and Today
Wilhelmina Harper
New York: E.P. Dutton 1983

Pilgrim Thanksgiving
Wilma P. Hays
New York: Coward McCann, 1955

*****Squanto and the First Thanksgiving**
Joyce K. Kessel
Minneapolis, MN: Carolrhoda Books, 1983

*****One Tough Turkey: A Thanksgiving Story**
Steven Kroll
New York: Holiday House, 1982

Thanksgiving Feast and Festival
Mildred C. Luckhardt
New York: Abingdon Press, 1966

*****It's Thanksgiving**
Jack Prelutsky
New York: Greenwillow Books, 1982

The Thanksgiving Treasure
Gail Rock
New York: Knopf, 1974

Food Sources

ACE PECAN CO.
P.O. Box 65
Cordele, GA 31015
(800) 323-9754
Nut of the Month Plan

AMERICAN SPOON FOODS
411 East Lake Street
Petoskey, MI 49770
(616) 347-9030
Morels

ASPEN MULLING SPICES
c/o Wax & Wicks, Inc.
P.O. Box 191
Aspen, CO 81612
Spice mix for mulled cider

BAINBRIDGE'S FESTIVE FOODS
P.O. Box 15805
Nashville, TN 37215
(615) 383-5157
Cranberry pineapple jelly, fig berry preserves

BALDUCCI'S
424 Avenue of the Americas
New York, NY 10011
(800) 228-2028, ext. 72
(212) 673-2600
Specialty foods

BRAE BEEF
THE NEW BUTCHER SHOP
Stamford Town Center
100 Greyrock Place
Stamford, CT 06901
(800) 323-4484
Preservative-free Beef

BUTTERFIELD FARMS
330-3 Washington Street
Marina del Rey, CA 90291
Fruitcake

CAMPBELL FARMS
P.O. Box 74
Post Mills, VT 05058
(802) 685-3813
Roast suckling pig

CALVERT CEDAR STREET INC.
3 South Fourth Street
Wilmington, NC 28401
(919) 763-9433
Pecan Vinaigrette

COMMONWEALTH ENTERPRISES LTD.
P.O. Box 49
Mongaup Valley, NY 12762
(914) 583-6630
Fresh foie gras

CZIMER FOODS
Route 7, Box 285
Lockport, IL 60441
(312) 460-2210
Game

D'ARTAGNAN INC.
399 St. Paul Avenue
Jersey City, NJ 07306
American foie gras, smoked duck

DEAN & DeLUCA
Mail-order Dept.
110 Greene Street
Suite 304
New York, NY 10012
(800) 221-7714
(212) 431-1691
Specialty foods

DIMPELMEIER BAKERY
Export Division
P.O. Box 192
Port Credit, Ontario L5G4L7
Canada
Breads

EILENBERGER'S BAKERY
512 North John Street
Palestine, TX 75801
(214) 729-2253
Pecan cake and fruitcake

THE FORST'S
CPO Box 1000P
12-24 Ten Broeck Avenue
Kingston, NY 12401
(800) 453-4010
(914) 331-3500
Game birds, beef, poultry, ham

GETHSEMANI FARMS
Highway 247
Trappist, KY 40051
(502) 549-3117
Trappist Fruitcake

GORDON-THOMPSON, LTD.
410 West Coast Highway
Newport Beach, CA 92663
(714) 645-5180
Wild game and exotic foods

THE LARDER OF LADY BUSTLE, LTD.
P.O. Box 53393
Atlanta, GA 30355
(404) 584-0525
Raisin Sauce, Brandied Cranberries

LATTA'S
P.O. Box 1377
Newport, OR 97365
(503) 265-7675
Smoked oysters, Indian Fry Bread Mix, Rhubarb-Apple Chutney

LAWRENCE'S SMOKE HOUSE
Route 30
RR#1, Box 28
Newfane, VT 05345
(802) 365-7751
Corncob-smoked ham

LINDEN BEVERAGE CO., INC.
Linden, VA 22642
(703) 635-5481
Alpenglow sparkling cider

MACY'S, THE CELLAR
151 West 34th Street
New York, NY 10001
(212) 695-4400
Specialty foods

MARKET SQUARE FOOD COMPANY
1642 Richfield
Highland Park, IL 60035
(312) 831-2228
(800) 232-2299
Chardonnay and Cabernet wine vinegars

MATTHEWS 1812 HOUSE INC.
15 Whitcomb Hill Road
Cornwall Bridge, CT 06754
(203) 672-0149
Fruit and nut cakes

McARTHUR'S SMOKEHOUSE, INC.
Main Street
Millerton, NY 12546
(518) 789-4425
Hickory-smoked poultry, ham

MEADOW FARMS COUNTRY
SMOKEHOUSE
P.O. Box 1387
2345 North Sierra Highway
Bishop, CA 93514
(619) 873-5311
Mahogany-smoked ham

METZ BAKING COMPANY
201 South Fifth
P.O. Box 457
Beatrice, NE 68310
(402) 223-2358
(800) 228-4030
Grandma's Master Fruitcake

NORTHERN LAKES WILD RICE
COMPANY
P.O. Box 28
Cass Lake, MN 56633
(218) 335-6369
June to November
P.O. Box 392
Teton Village, WY 83025
(307) 733-7192
December to May
Wild rice

OAKWOOD GAME FARM
Box 274
Princeton, MN 55371
(800) 328-6647
(612) 389-2077
Game birds

PAN HANDLER PRODUCTS
4580 Maple Street
Waterbury Center, VT 05677
(802) 244-5597
Cranapple Maple Conserves

PINNACLE ORCHARDS
441 South Fir
Medford, OR 97501
(800) 547-0227
Fruit

POLLY JEAN'S PANTRY
4561 Mission Gorge Place
Suite K
San Diego, CA 92120
(619) 283-5429
(800) 621-0852, ext. 289
Sauce a L'orange, St. Ives Relish, Chutney

ROWENA'S AND CAPTAIN JAAP'S
758 West 22nd Street
Norfolk, VA 23517
(804) 627-8699
Cranberry Nut Conserve

SARABETH'S KITCHEN
423 Amsterdam Avenue
New York, NY 10024
(212) 496-6280
Cranberry Relish

S.E. RYCOFF & COMPANY
P.O. Box 21467
Los Angeles, CA 90021
Specialty foods

SMITHFIELD HAM & PRODUCTS CO.
P.O. Box 487
Smithfield, VA 23430
(800) 628-2242
(804) 357-2121
Ham

THE SOCIETY BAKERY
Box 877
104 Charles Street
Boston, MA 02114
(617) 648-4695
Fruit and nut cakes

TIMBER CREST FARMS
4791 Dry Creek Road
Healdsburg, CA 95448
(707) 433-8251
Dried fruit and nuts

VERMONT'S CLEARVIEW FARMS
RR#1
Enosburg Falls, VT 05450
(802) 933-2537
Cranberry Relish

VIEUX CARRE FOODS INC.
P.O. Box 26956
New Orleans, LA 70186
(504) 525-3880
Creole Praline Sauce

S. WALLACE EDWARDS & SONS, INC.
Box 25
Surry, VA 23883
(804) 294-3121
(800) 222-4267
Ham

WILLIAMS-SONOMA
5750 Hollis Street
Emeryville, CA 94608
(415) 652-1555
Specialty foods

WOODLAND PANTRY
Forest Foods, Inc.
138 Wright Lane
Oak Park, IL 60302
(312) 848-3144
Wild mushrooms

YORK HARBOR EXPORT, INC.
P.O. Box 737
Varrell Lane
York Harbor, ME 03911
Belon oysters

Index

Page numbers in italics refer to illustrations and sidebars. Titles of recipes are in italics, and titles of poems and songs are in quotation marks.

A

Abe de la Houssaye's Corn Bread and Jalpeño Dressing, 95
Acorn Squash, 75
Activities for fun, 30-33
Adolphus, Don, 144
Alain Sailhac's Eggplant and Spinach Cake, 94
Alcott, Luisa May, 124-135
Allen, Steve, 60
"America the Beautiful," 113
American Museum of Natural History, 41, 48
American Revolution, Thanksgiving days during, 13
Andree's-Mediterranean's Baba Ghannoush, 96
Andy the Alligator balloon, 54
Anglo-Saxon Harvest Home, 12
Apple and prune stuffing, roast goose with, 73
Apple gratiné with cranberries, 96
Applejack, duck breasts cooked in, 77
Apples
   duck breasts with, 77
   gratiné, with cranberries, 96
   stuffing, roast goose with, 73
Applesauce, 85
Arapaho Indians, mealtime prayer of, 142
Artichokes, steamed, 86

B

Baba Ghannoush, 96
Bacon, ragout of, 96
Balloons, in Macy's Thanksgiving Day Parade, 44, 46-55
Bands, in Macy's Thanksgiving Day Parade, 63
Bates, Katherine Lee, 113
Bedtime Bear float, 57
Ben Franklin float, 58

Bert Greene's Pumpkin Burnt Cream, 95
Betty Boop balloon, 46, 53
Big Bad Wolf balloon, 54
Bird Hash, 90
Birthday Bear float, 57
Black-eyed Peas with Ham and Red Peppers, 83
Bliss, Henry, 136
Bourgeois, Louis, 140
Bradford, William, 23
Brandied compote, 32
Brandy, fruits in, 93
Bread Pudding, 90
Broccoli Puree, 71
Broiled Shad Roe, 75
Brussels sprouts, on harvest table, 31
Brussels Sprouts and Malt Vinegar, 83
Bullwinkle the Moose balloon, 46
Burns, Robert, 152
Burpee Seed Company, 27

C

Cabbage Patch Kids float, 56
Caesar, Sid, 60
Candles, decorated, 108
Canning, Josian Dean, 152
Cara, Irene, 60
Care Bears float, 56, 57
Celebrities, in Macy's Thanksgiving Day Parade, 60-63
Central Park, 41
Cerelia, Roman festival of, 12
Ceres (Roman goddess), 12
Chamberlin, Clarence, 54
Chanterelles, wild rice with, 68
Charm Strings, 27
Cheddar cheese, *79*
Cheer Bear float, 57
Cheese and Fruit, 79
Chestnuts
   on harvest table, 31
   ragout of, with onions and bacon, 96
   roasted, 32
   in stuffing, 81
Children's Place Setting, 103
Chives, wild rice with chanterelles and, 68
Cider, duck breasts cooked in, 77

Clark, Dick, 60
Coca, Imogene, 60
Colquitt County High School Band, *62*
"Come, Ye Thankful People, Come," 119
Compote, 32, 93
Corn, Indian, 29
Corn Bread, Chestnut, and Sausage Stuffing, 81
Corn bread and jalapeno dressing, 95

D

Dakota (apartment building), 41
Decorated Candle, 108
Deglazing, *67*
Deluise, Dom, 63
Demeter (Greek goddess), 12
Deviled Oyster Stew, 83
Dieter Schorner's Apple Gratiné with Cranberries, 96
Disney, Walt, 54
Disneyland celebration floats, 57
Domingo, Placido, 63
Donald Duck balloon, 46
Doodlebug float, 57, *57*
Douglas, Marian, 147
"Down in My Heart," 141
"Doxology, The," 140
Dressing, corn bread and jalapeno, 95
Dried flowers, 27-29
Drunken Pound Cake, 93
Duck hearts in pumpkin soup, 95
Duck Breasts with Apples Cooked in Cider and Applejack, 77

E

Eggplant
   baba ghannoush, 96
   and spinach cake, 94
Eisenhower, Dwight D., 16
Elrey, G. J., 119
Elsie the cow balloon, 46
Emerson, Nanette Snow, 138-139

F

Feast of St. Martin of Tours, 12

"Feast-Time of the Year, The," 136
Felix the cat balloon, 53
Fisher, Eddie, 60
Flintstone, Fred, *61*
Float Centerpiece, 103
Floats, in Macy's Thanksgiving Day Parade, 40, 56-60
Flowers, dried, 27-29
Fresh Cranberry Relish, 68
Fried Oysters, 75
Friend Bear float, 57
Fruit, cheese and, 79
Fruits in Brandy, 93
Funshine Bear float, 57

G

Gale, Norman, 146
Garfield the Cat balloon, 46, 48, *48-49*, 53
Garlic Potatoes, 70
George Washington float, 58
Gingerbread, 86
"Giving Thanks," 115
Glazed Ham, 85
Gleason, Jackie, *61*
Gobler the Turkey balloon, 54
Godey's Lady's Book, 14, *16*
Good Luck Bear float, 57
"Good Thanksgiving, A," 147
Goodman, Benny, 60
Goose, with apple and prune stuffing, 73
Gourds, 26-27, *27*, 105
Grapefruit, lettuce salad with, 70
Gratiné, apple, with cranberries, 96
Gravlax, 96
Greece, ancient, festival in, 12
Grumpy Bear float, 57
Gruyere, spoonbread with ham and, 90
Gulf and Western Building, 41
Gurney Seed and Nursery Company, *27*

H

Hale, Sarah Josepha, 14
Ham
  black-eyed peas with, 83
  glazed, 85
  spoonbread with, and gruyere, 90
Harvest table, 31
"Hebrew Morning Service, The," 143
Hemans, Felicia D., 114
Herald Square, 41, 44
Holm, Celeste, 60
Hope, Bob, 60
Horace Horse Collar Balloon, 54

I

Indian corn, 29

Indian Pudding, 75
International Year of the Child, 53

J

Jalapeño and corn bread dressing, 95
James Beard's Quince Tart, 97
Jean-Louis Palladin's Pumpkin Soup with Preserved Duck Hearts and Gizzards, 95
Jerusalem Artichokes, 75
Jewish prayer, 143

K

Kaye, Danny, 60
Ken, Thomas, 140
Kermit the frog balloon, 46, *52*, 53, 54

L

La Guardia, Fiorello, 37
"Landing of the Pilgrim Fathers, The," 114
Lawrence, Bessie, 116-118
Leeks, creamed, with onions, 68
Lennon, John, 41
"Let Us Break Bread Together," 122
Lettuce Salad with Grapefruit, 70
Lincoln, Abraham, 14, 16
LIncoln Tunnel, 58
Lobster Caesar Salad, 77
Love-A-Lot Bear float, 57
Lydie Marshall's Ragout of Onions, Bacon, and Chestnuts, 96

M

McMahon, Ed, *61*
Macy's Special Productions Department, 40
Macy's Thanksgiving Day parade, 8, 30, 34-45
  balloons in, 44, 46-55
  bands in, 63
  best viewing spots for, 42
  celebrities in, 60-63
  floats in, 56-60
  history of, 36-39
  planning for, 40
  route of, 41
  tips for spectators, 44
Madison, James, 13
Majestic Apartments, 41
Malt vinegar, brussels sprouts and, 83
Marriot Marquis Hotel, 42
Marx, Harpo, 60
Massasoit (Indian), 23, *24*, 25
Masters of the Universe float, 56-57

Mayflower, 22
Mayflower Hotel, 42
Mayonnaise, 78
Mickey Mouse balloon, 46, *50*, 54
Middle Ages, festival in, 12
Miller, Ann, *61*
Mincemeat, 93
Miracle on 34th Street, A (movie), 40, 60
Morels in Butter, 75
Mrs. Rocking Kangaroo float, 60

N

NBC, Macy's Thanksgiving Day Parade broadcast on, 37
New Amsterdam Dutch, 13
New England, early Thanksgiving celebrations in, 13-14
New York Coliseum, 41
New York Convention and Visitors Bureau, 42
New York Historical Society, 41
Noah's Ark float, 57
Novotel, 42

O

Old Sturbridge Village, 18, *19*
"Old-Fashioned Thanksgiving, An" (excerpt), 124-135
Olive Oyl balloon, 48
"One Thanksgiving," 138-139
Onions
  creamed, with leeks, 68
  ragout, with bacon and chestnuts, 96
O'Hara, Maureen, 60
Oranges, in salad, with shrimp and apples, 90
"Over the River," 121
Oysters, 75, 83

P

Paddington Bear float, *57*
Pancetta, red cabbage with, 77
Parade, *see* Macy's Thanksgiving Day Parade
Park Seed Company, *27*
Payne, John, 60
Pear-and-Cranberry Compote, 93
Pecan-Sweet Potato Pie, 83
Perla Meyers' Cointreau Cranberry Preserves, 96
Pie
  pecan-sweet potato, 83
  pumpkin chiffon, 71
Pilgrim Dolls, 106
Pilgim float, 58
Pilgrim Place, 18

Index

Pilgrims, 12-13, 20-25
Pillows, turkey applique, 100
Placemats, wheat, 109
Plimouth Plantation, 18
Plymouth, Massachusetts, 12-13, 20-25
Poached Vegetables in Vinaigrette, 78
Pomander Balls, 104
Popeye balloon, 54
Potatoes
    garlic, 70
    scalloped, 77
    twice-baked, 85
Potpourri Gourds, 105
"Prayer before Eating," 142
Preserves, cranberry, 96
Prune and apple stuffing, roast goose with, 73
Pumpkin burnt cream, 95
Pumpkin Chiffon Pie, 71
Pumpkin soup, 95
Puritans (Pilgrims), 13, 20-25

Q

Queen Elizabeth II, 53
Quince tart, 97

R

Raggedy Ann balloon, 48, *48,* 53
Ragout of onions, bacon, and chestnuts, 96
Rainbow Brite float, 56
Recipes, 66-97
Red Cabbage with Pancetta, 77
Red peppers, black-eyed peas and ham with, 83
Relish, cranberry, 68
Richard Lavin's Gravlax, 96
Richard Lavin's Stuffed Snow Peas, 94
Roast Capon, 81
Roast Goose with Apple and Prune Stuffing, 73
Roast Turkey and Gravy, 67
Roasted chestnuts, 32
Robotman & Friends float, 58
Rockettes (dance company), 60, *61*
Rogers, Ginger, 60
Rome, ancient, festival in, 12
Roosevelt, Franklin Delano, 16
Ruggles, Charlie, 60

S

St. George's Windsor, 119
Samoset (Indian), 22-23, *24,* 25
Santa Claus balloon, 54
Santa Claus float, 56, 57, 60
Sarg, Tony, 53, *53*
Sausage stuffing, 81

Scalloped Potatoes, 77
Shad roe, broiled, 75
Sheaves, 27-29
Shrimp, Orange, and Apple Salad, 90
Shrimp with Curry Mayonnaise, 77
"Simple Gifts," 151
Smokey the Bear baloon, *54-55*
Snoopy balloon, 46, 48
Snow peas, stuffed, 94
Soup Stock, 90
Spinach and eggplant cake, 94
Spoonbread with Ham and Gruyere, 90
Squanto (Indian), *22, 23, 24,* 25
Squash, acorn, 75
Standish, Miles, 22, 25
Statue of Liberty float, 57
Steamed Artichokes, 86
Stuffing, 67, 73, 81
Sukkoth, 12
Superman balloon, 46,48, *51, 53*
Sweet potato and pecan pie, 83

T

Tenderheart Bear float, 57
Texas Tofee, 93
"Thanks," 146
"Thanksgiving," 116-118
Thanksgiving
    first celebration of, 12-13, 20-25
    historical celebrations of, 10-19
"Thanksgiving: A Poem in Two Parts" (excerpt), 136
Thanksgiving constitutional, 33
"Thanksgiving Day," 144
Thanksgiving Day Parade, *see* Macy's Thanksgiving Day Parade
"Thanksgiving Eve" (excerpt), 152
Thanksgiving meals, 66-97
"Thanksgiving Time," 136
Times Square, 41
Toast, progressive Thanksgiving, 33
Tootsie Roll float, 56
Traditions to establish, 30-33
Truman, Harry S, 16
Turkey
    roast, 67
    thawing of, 71
    tidbits about, 73
    timetable for roasting, 68
    tips on, 68
Turkey Applique Pillow, 100
"Turkey in the Straw," 148
Twice-baked Potatoes, 85

U

Underdog balloon, 46, 54
U.S. Marines Drum and Bugle Corps, *62*

V

Vermont cheddar, *79*
Vinaigrette, poached vegetables in, 78
Vinegars, 93

W

Ward, Samuel A., 113
Warwick, Dionne, 63
Washington, George, 13
West Park Hotel, 42
Wheat, 29
Wheat Basket Centerpiece, 101
Wheat Placemats, 109
Wild Rice with Chanterelles and Fresh Chives, 68
Winchester Community High School Band, *62*
Wish Bear float, 57
Woody Woodpecker balloon, 46, 48

Y

Yogi Bear balloon, 48, *48*

Photo Credits

Cenicola, Tony: 79(t), 88, 100, 101(t)(b), 102, 104(t)(b) 105, 107, 108, 109

Consulate General of the Netherlands: 15, 21

Contempo: 77

Dos Passos, Manuel: 129, 134, 147, 150

Dos Passos, Sandra: 26, 29(br), 117, 133, 138, 143, 144-145

Duane, Susan: 112

Foti, Arthur: 27(l), 135, 136(b), 152

Glasgow, Keith: 85

Howard, Jerry/Positive Images: 28, 29(tr), 33(t), 70, 137

Klein, Matthew: 12, 69, 74, 78, 81, 82, 87, 89, 92, 95, 96-97

Leatart, Brian: 66

Lenox China: 83

Lyon, Fred/Wheeler Pictures: 31(l)(r), 32, 79(r), 86

Macy's Debustibus Cooking School: 94

© R.H. Macy & Co., Inc., New York
Courtesy of Macy's Thanksgiving Day Parade

    p. 36: Archive 1931
    p. 37: Archive 1928
    p. 38: Archive 1948
    p. 39: (t) Archive 1928
         (b) Archive 1926
    p. 40: (t) Archive N.D.
         (b) 1985
    p. 41: (t) 1982
         (b) 1985
    p. 42: Ira Shore 1985
    p. 43: 1984
    p. 44: (l) Thomas Trengove 1985
    p. 45: 1984, Cisco Junior College, Texas
    p. 46: 1977
    p. 47: 1982, Centerville Ohio High School Band, Ohio
    p. 48: (t) Thomas Trengove, 1984
         (b) Thomas Trengove, Raggedy Ann balloon©1984, Character Licensing, Inc.
    p. 49: Thomas Trengove 1985
    p. 50: (tl) 1985
         (tr) 1984
         (bl) 1934
         (br) 1984
    p. 51: Archive 1959
    p. 52: John Scheiber 1982
    p. 53: Archive 1931
    p. 54: Archive 1932
    p. 55: 1978

p. 56: 1984
p. 57: (t) 1984
     (b) 1984
p. 58: (l) 1985
     (r) 1985
p. 59: 1982
p. 60: (t) 1982
     (b) 1979
p. 60-61: (t) Archive 1952
        (b) 1979
p. 61: (t) 1981
     (b) 1982
p. 62: (t) 1979, Winchester Community High School, Indiana
     (c) 1979, Coloquitt County High School, Moultrie, Georgia
     (b) 1977, U.S. Marines Drum and Bugle Corps, Washington, D.C.
p. 63: 1982

New York Public Library, picture collection: 9, 14, 22-23, 24 (t), 114-115, 120, 124-125, 126-127, 149

Old Sturbridge Village: 19, 72

O'Rourke, Randy: 20, 24(b), 68, 73, 76, 123, 130, 146

Paige, Peter: 67, 80

Parker, Bo: p. 27(r)

Perron, Robert: 29(l), 128, 131, 132, 141, 153

Plimoth Plantation: 13, 16, 17, 18, 22, 23, 142

Rothschild, Bill: 90

Soloman, Paul/Wheeler Pictures: 79(b), 84

Tenzer, Peter/Wheeler Pictures: 33(b)

Weleman, Hans/Wheeler Pictures: 140

Weiss, Jeffery: 136(t)

Props for the photographs on pages 12, 69, 74, 78, 81, 82, 87, 89, 92, 95, 96-97 and the cover were supplied by:

Gordon Foster   1322 Third Avenue   New York, New York

Pierre Deux   369 Bleeker   New York, New York

Baccarat   55 East 57th Street   New York, New York

Cerelene   55 East 57th Street   New York, New York

Swid Powell   55 East 57th Street   New York, New York

Buccellati Silver   46 East 57th Street   New York, New York

Very Special Flowers   215 West 10th Street   New York, New York